Chapter 1
Orbleue's

Chapter 2
Jenny Wei

Chapter 3
Twisted Branch Studio

Chapter 4
Linda Karpinski

Chapter 5
Faith Swann

Chapter 6
Amandine Cyril ML

Chapter 7
Mr End

Chapter 8
Fabienne Tosi

Chapter 9
Lynni Ex

Chapter 10
T.J.

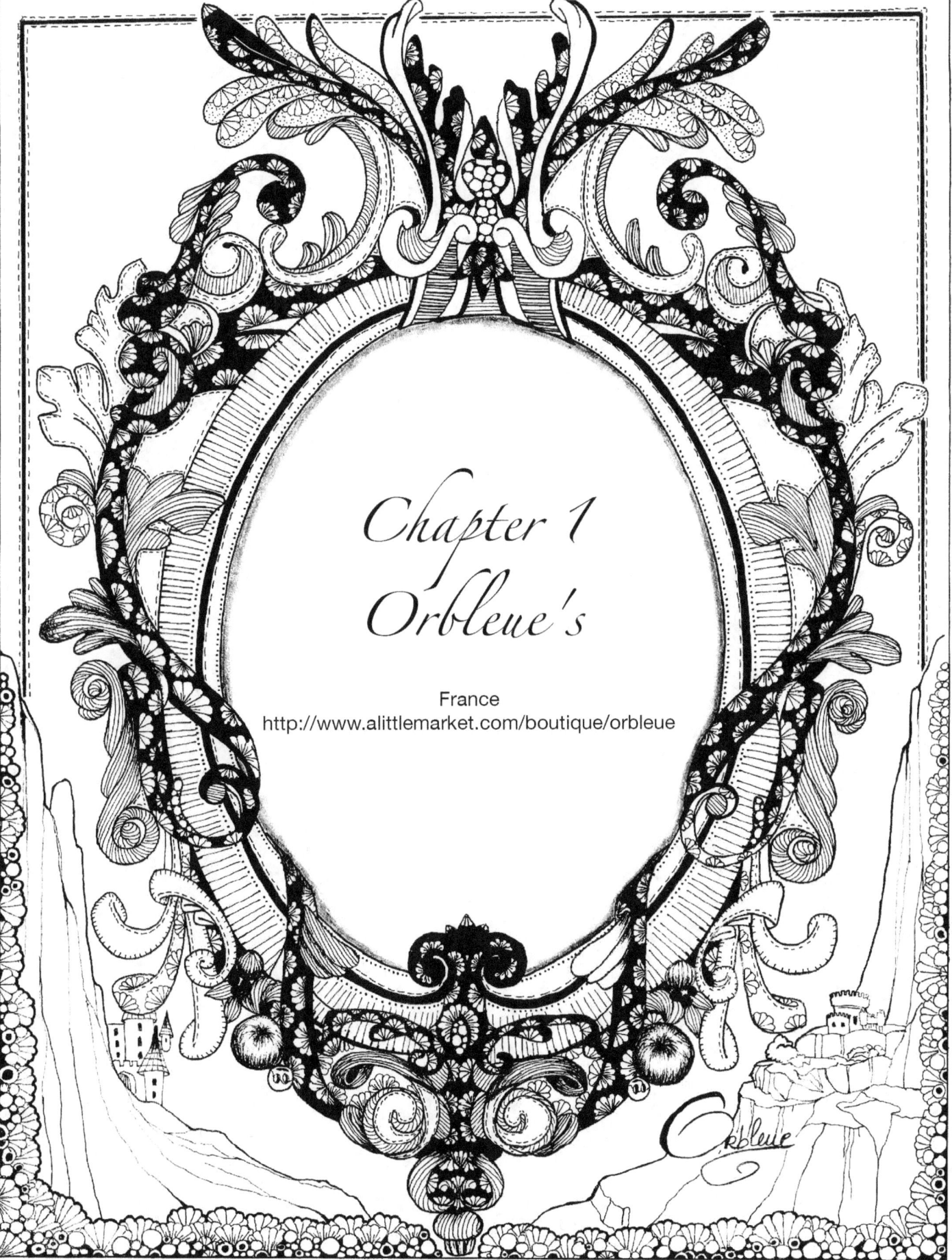

Chapter 1
Orbleue's

France
http://www.alittlemarket.com/boutique/orbleue

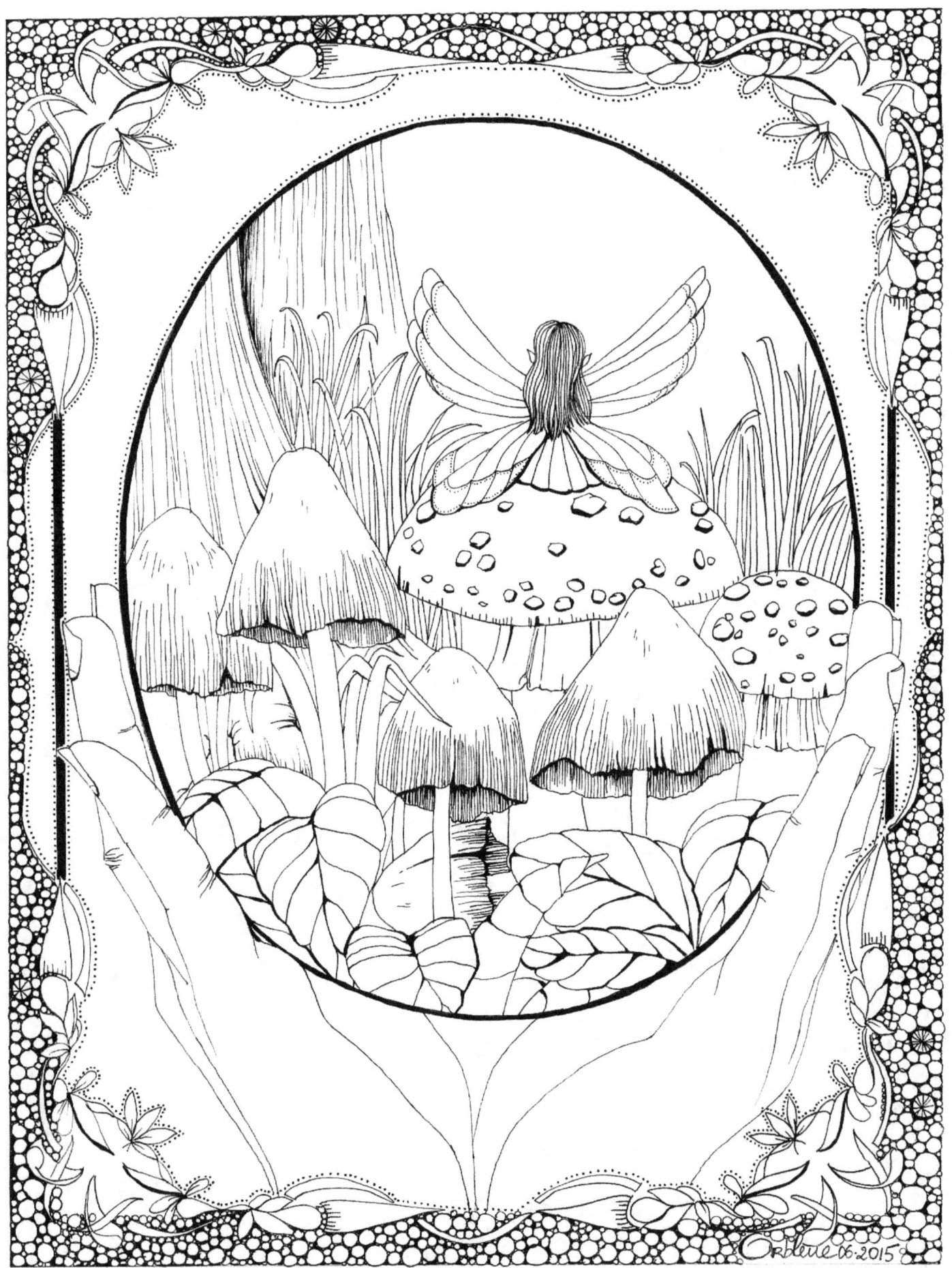

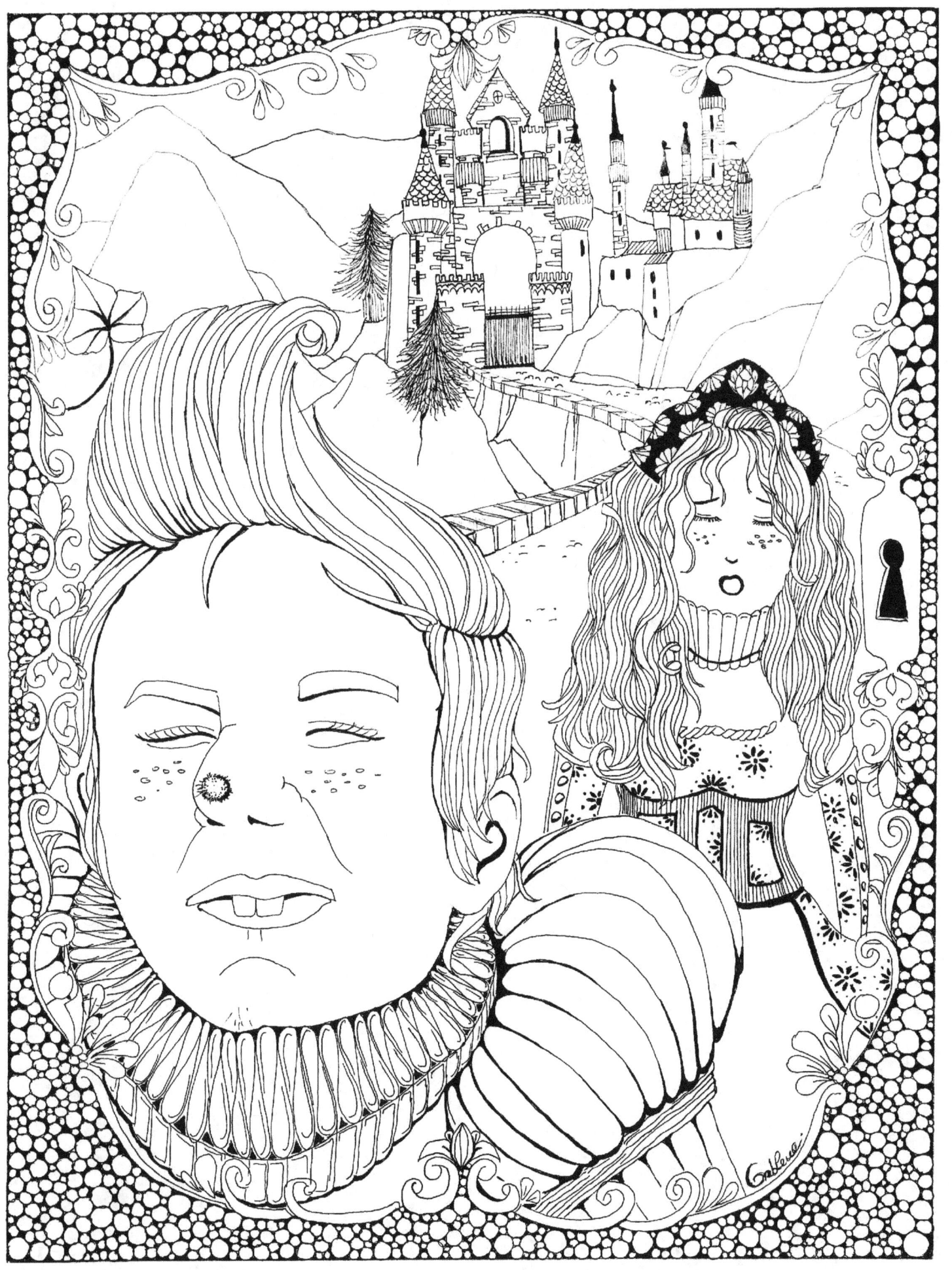

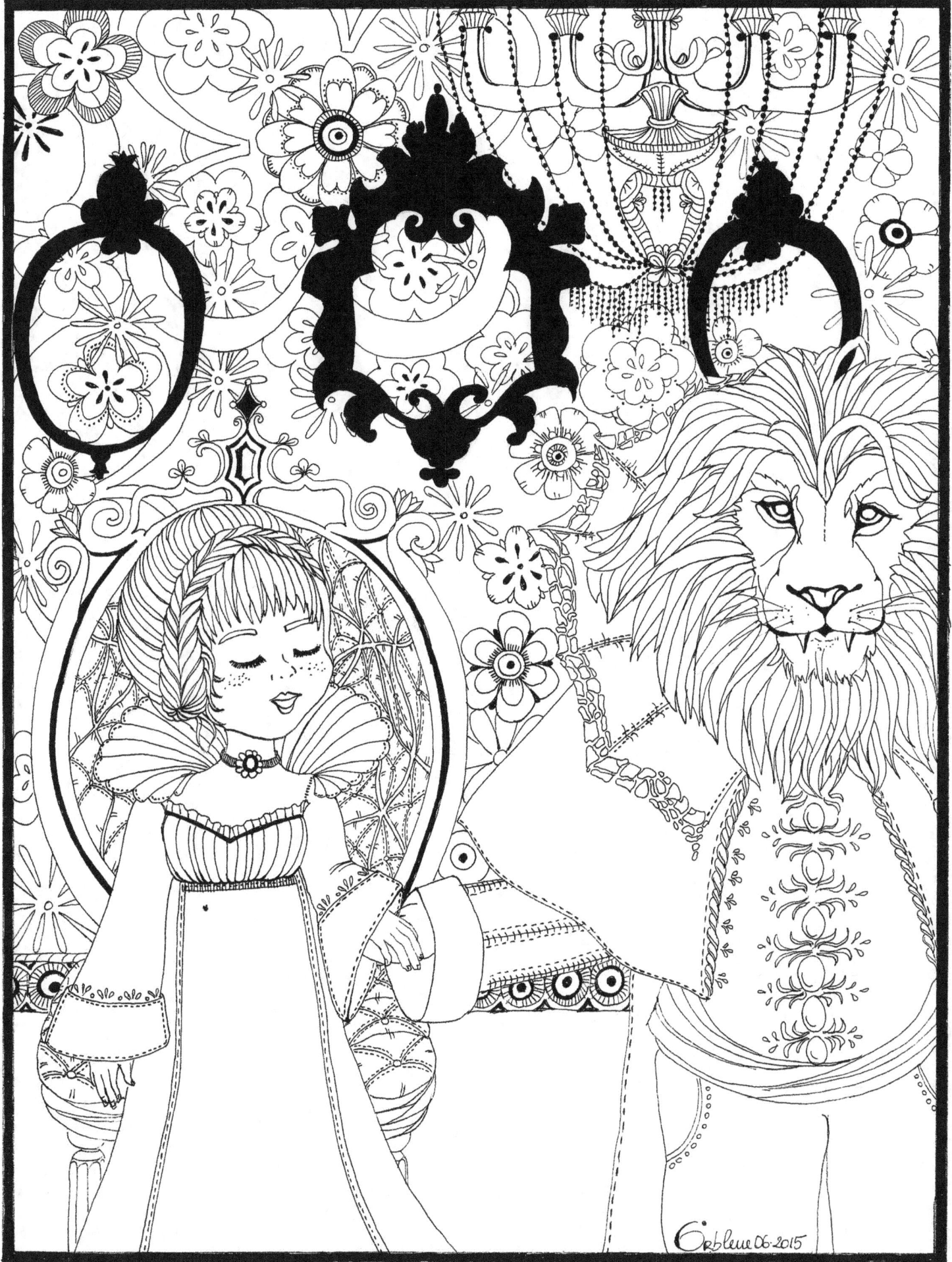

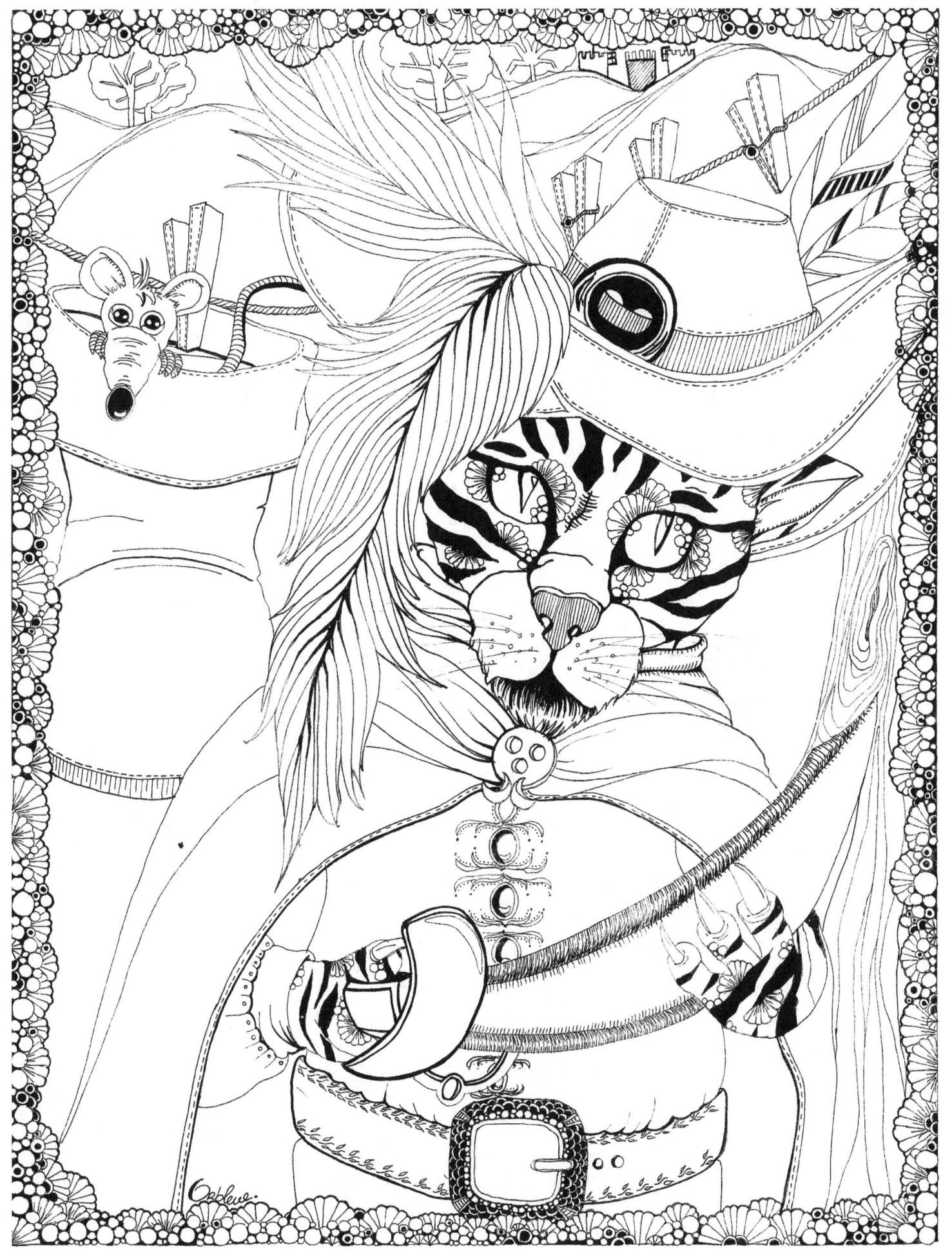

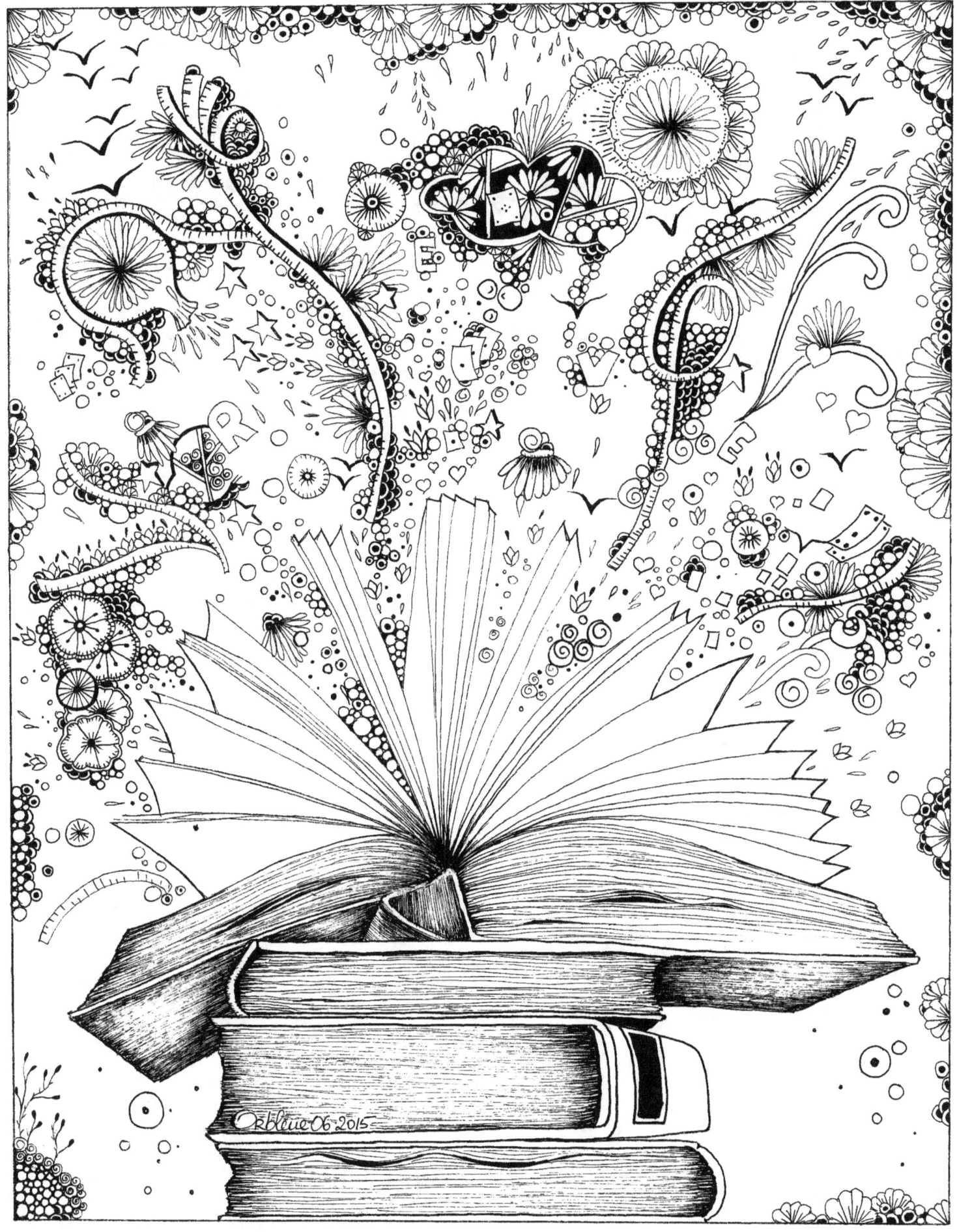

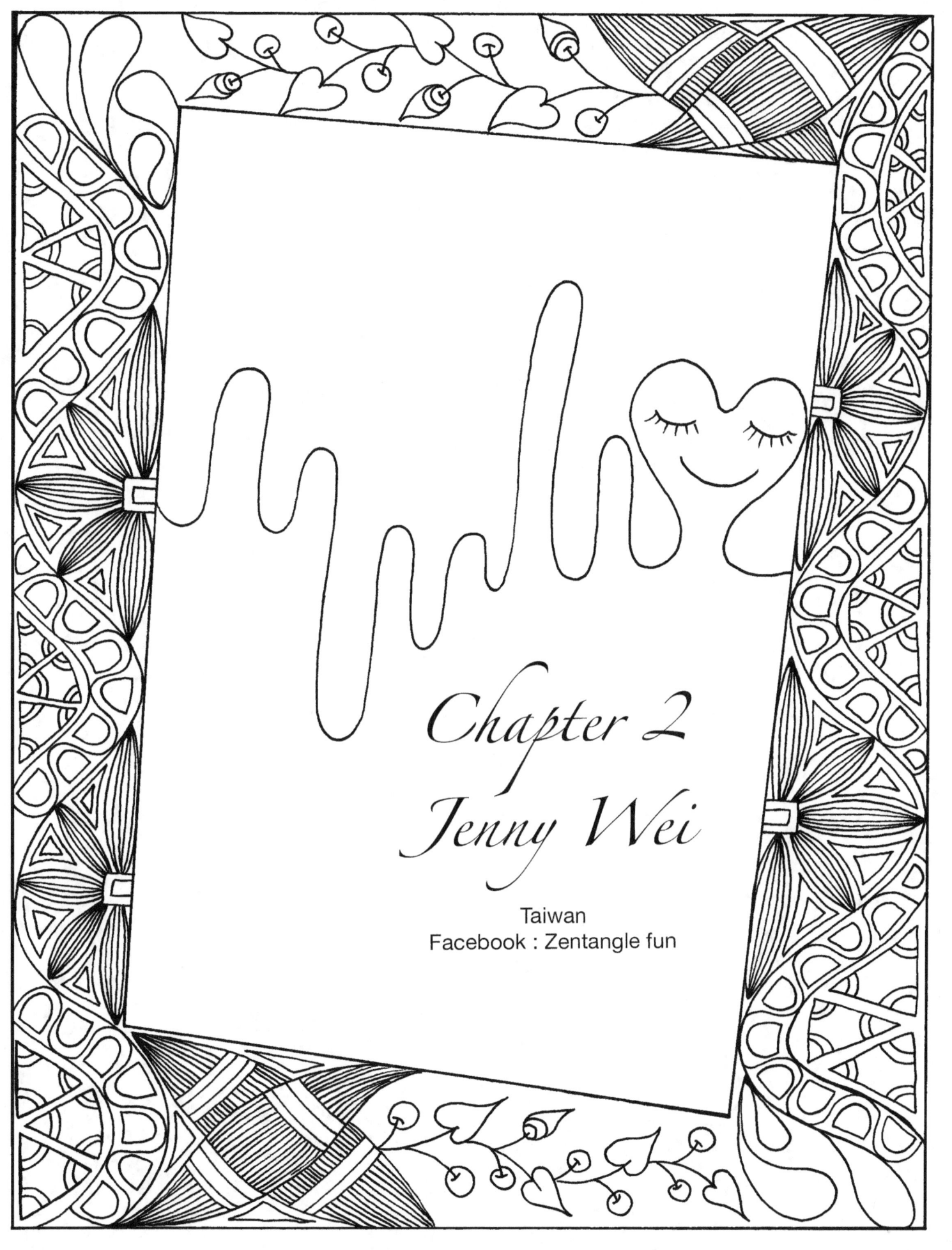

Chapter 2
Jenny Wei

Taiwan
Facebook : Zentangle fun

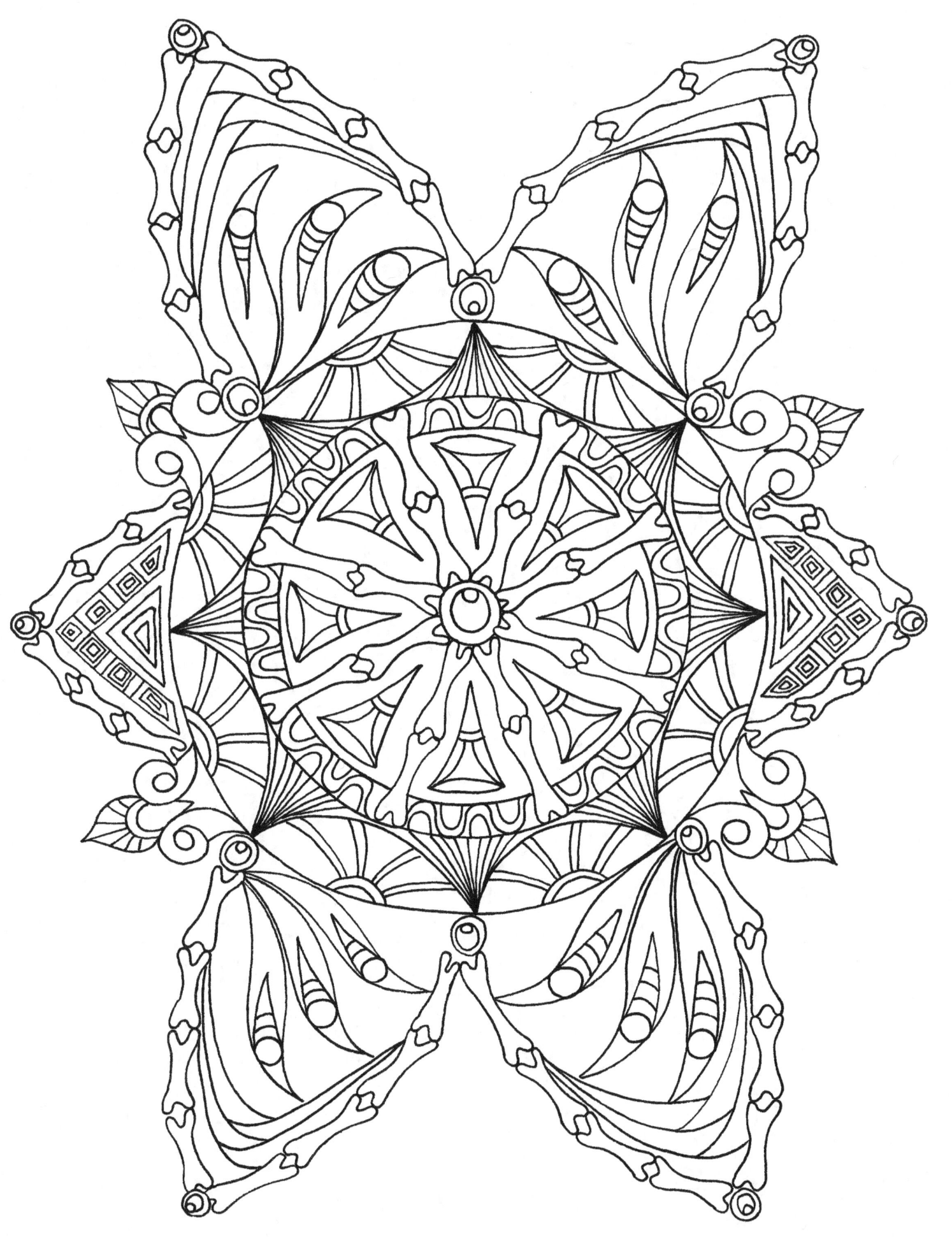

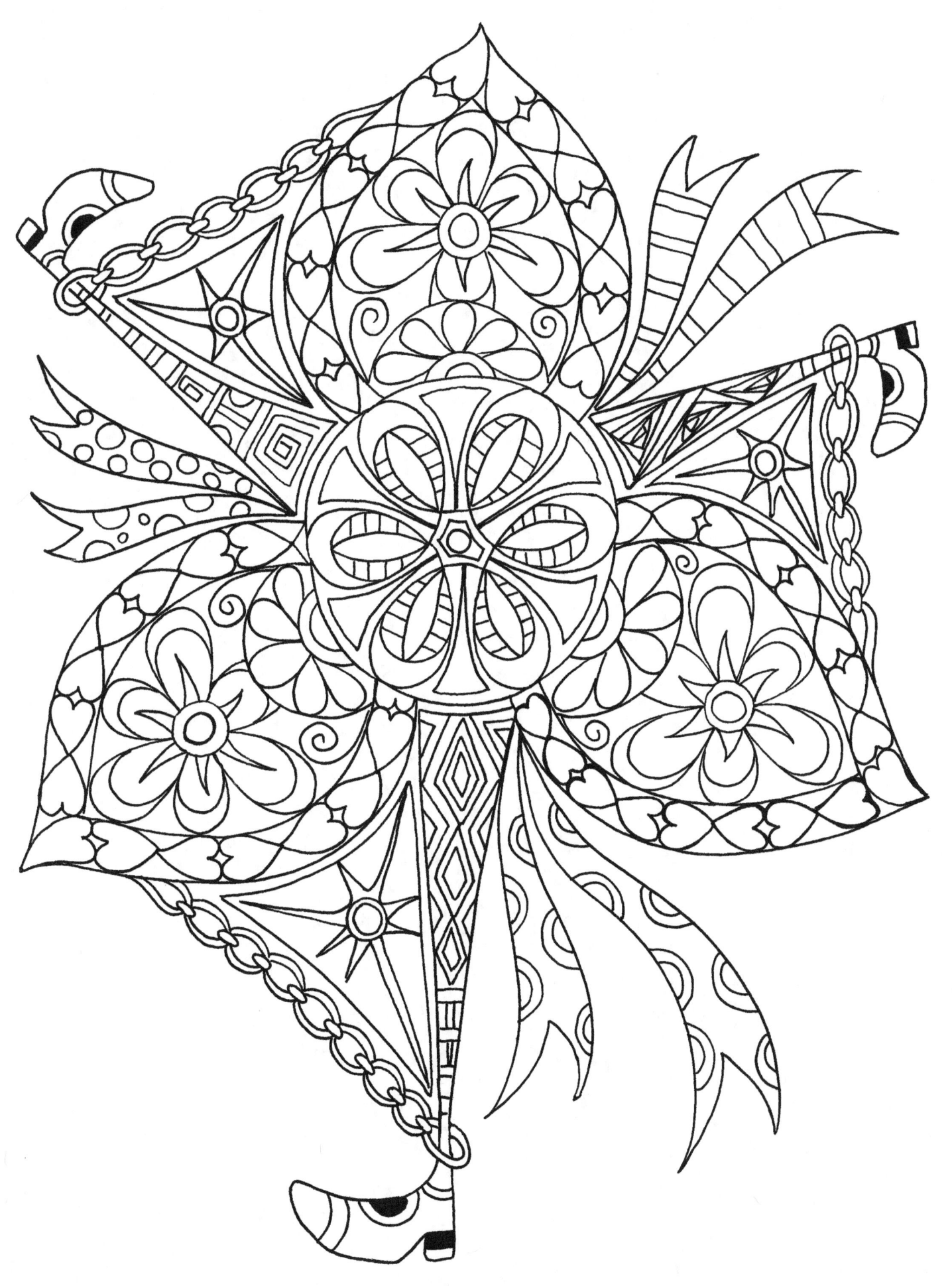

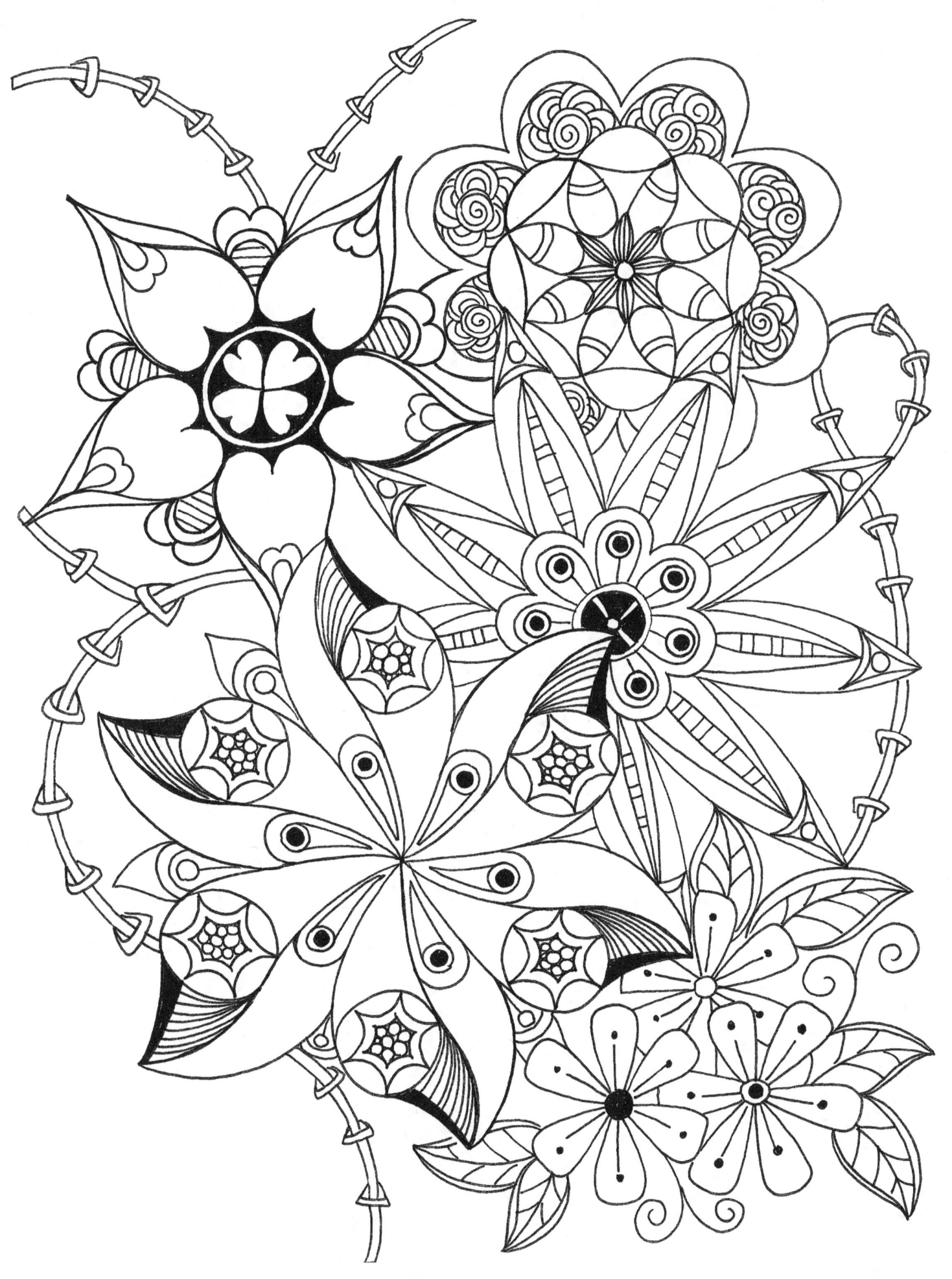

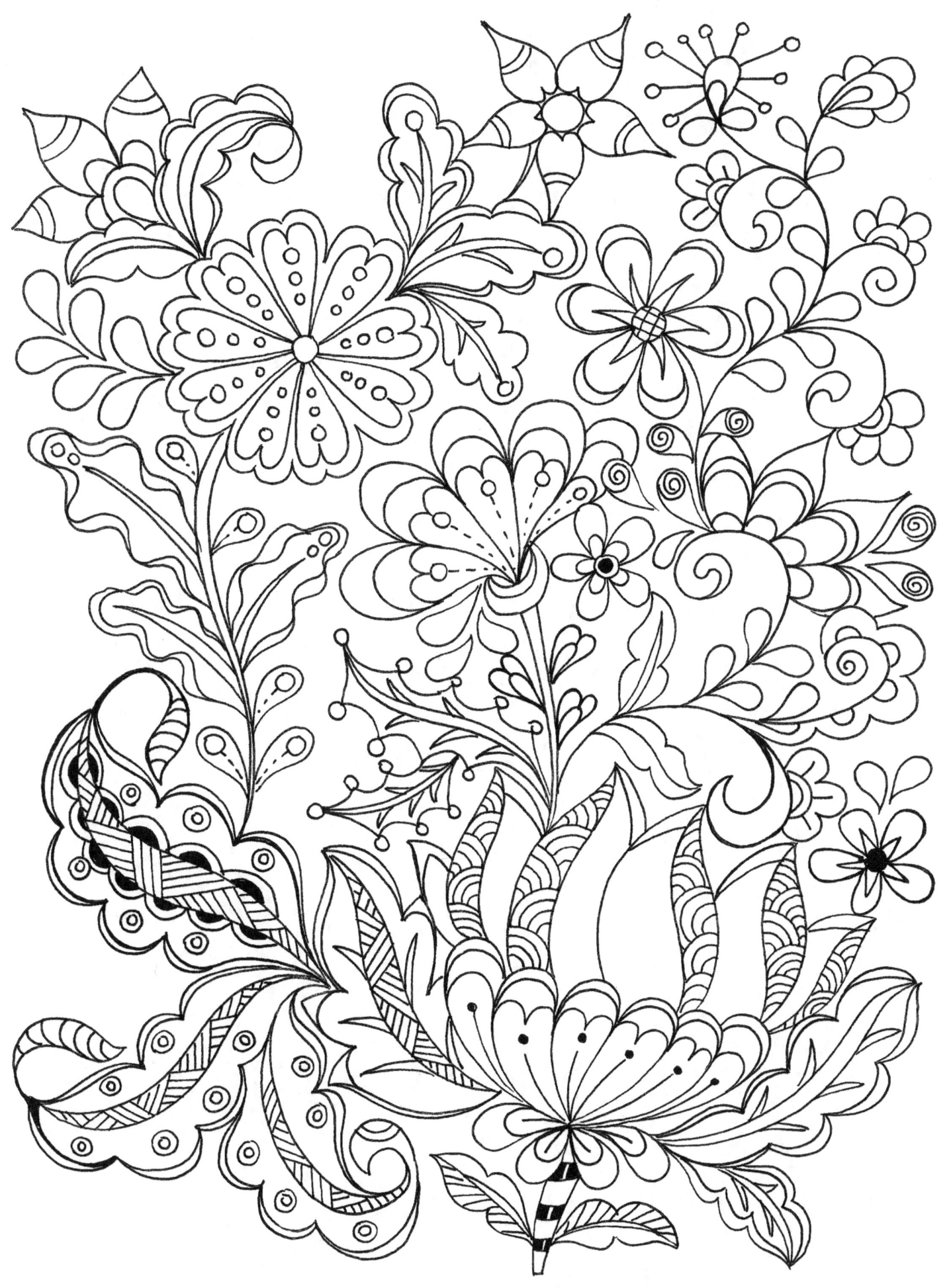

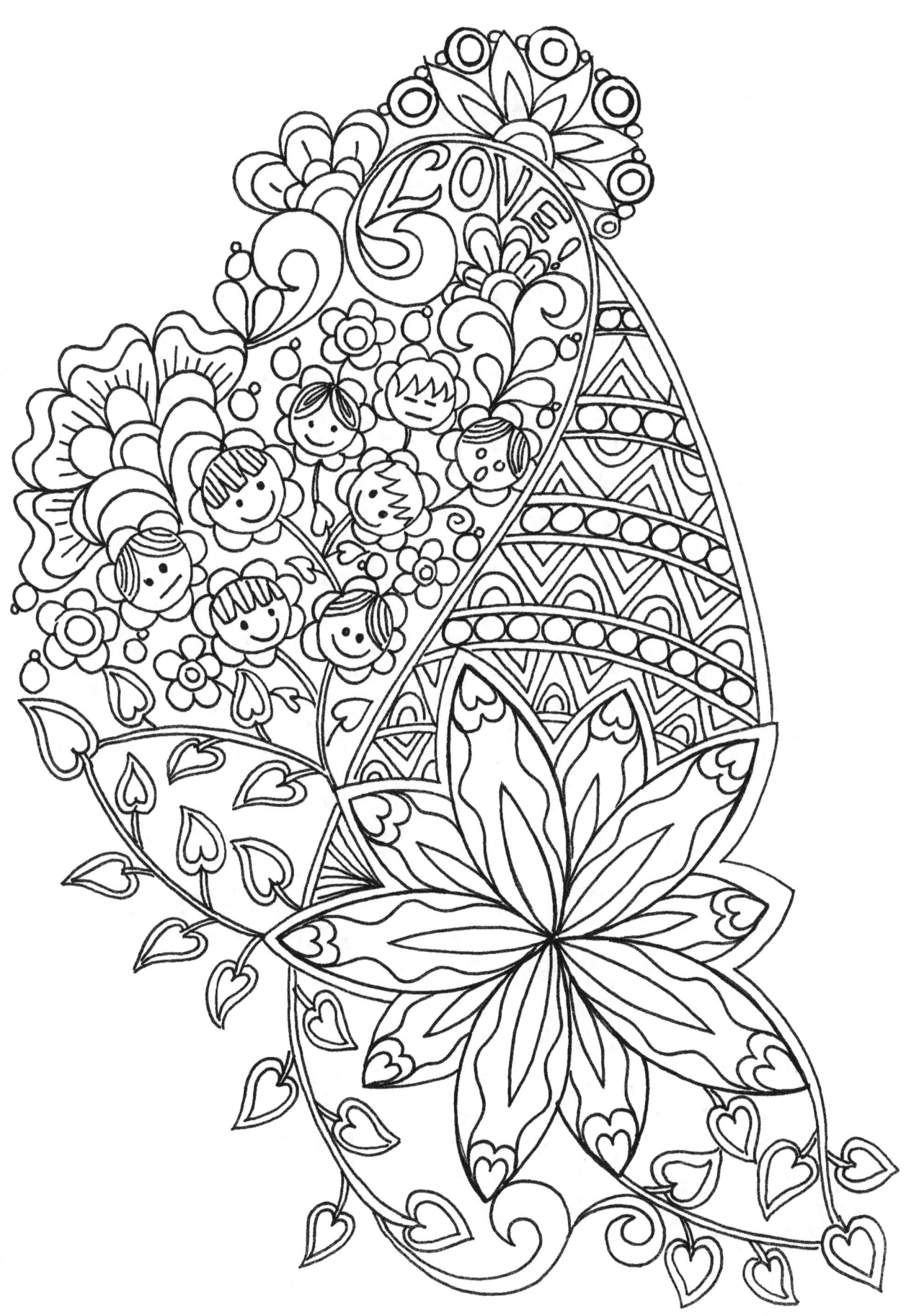

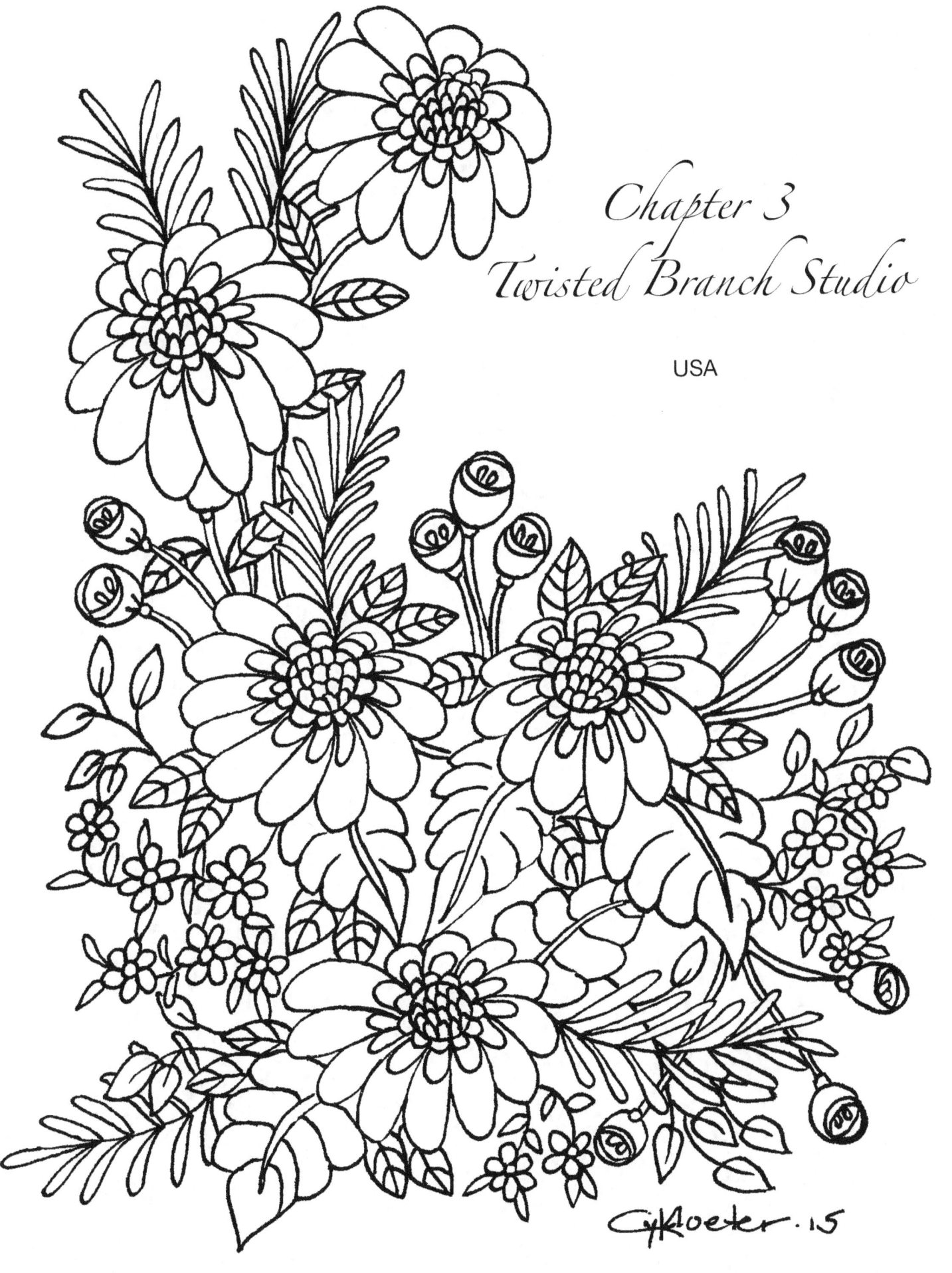

Chapter 3
Twisted Branch Studio

USA

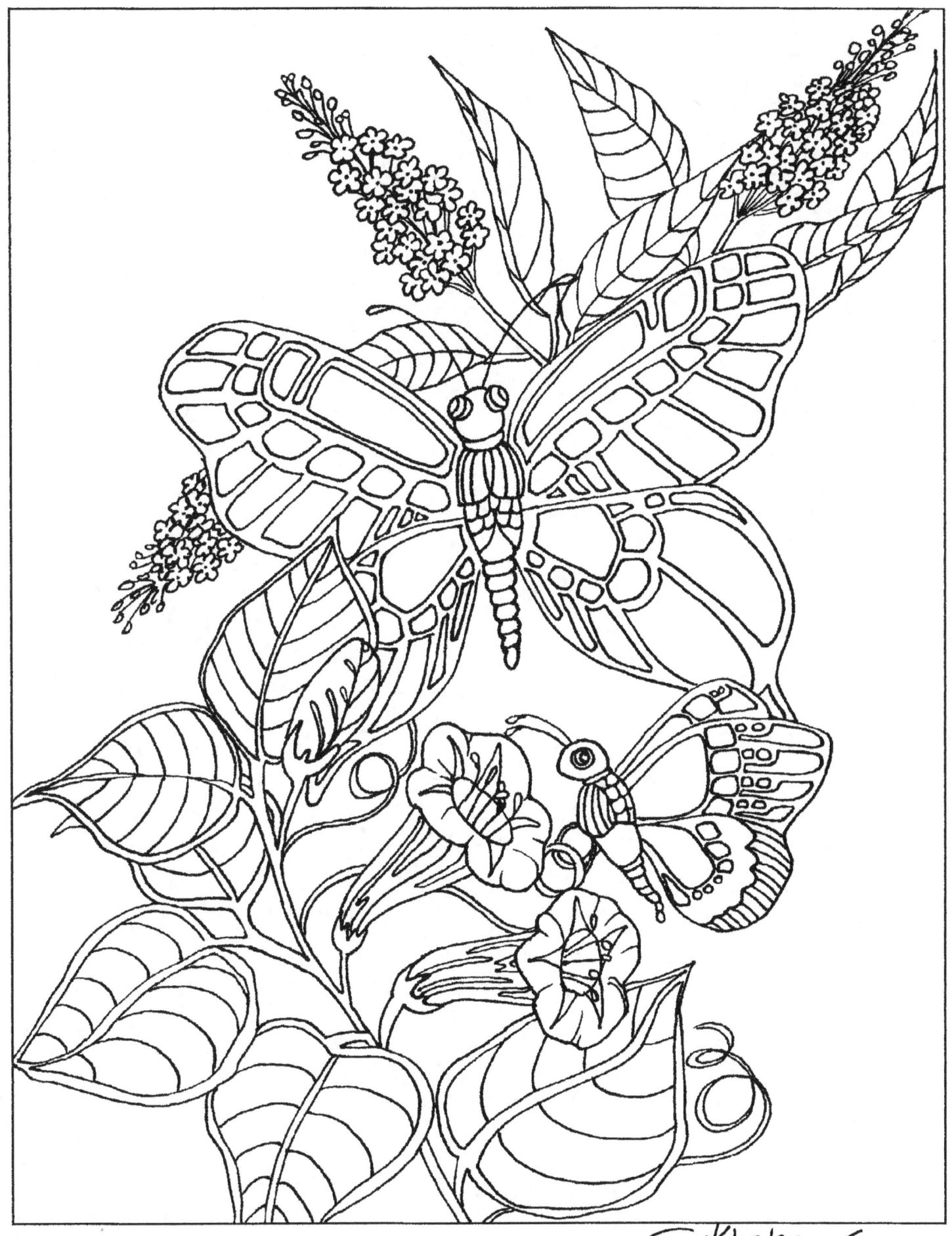

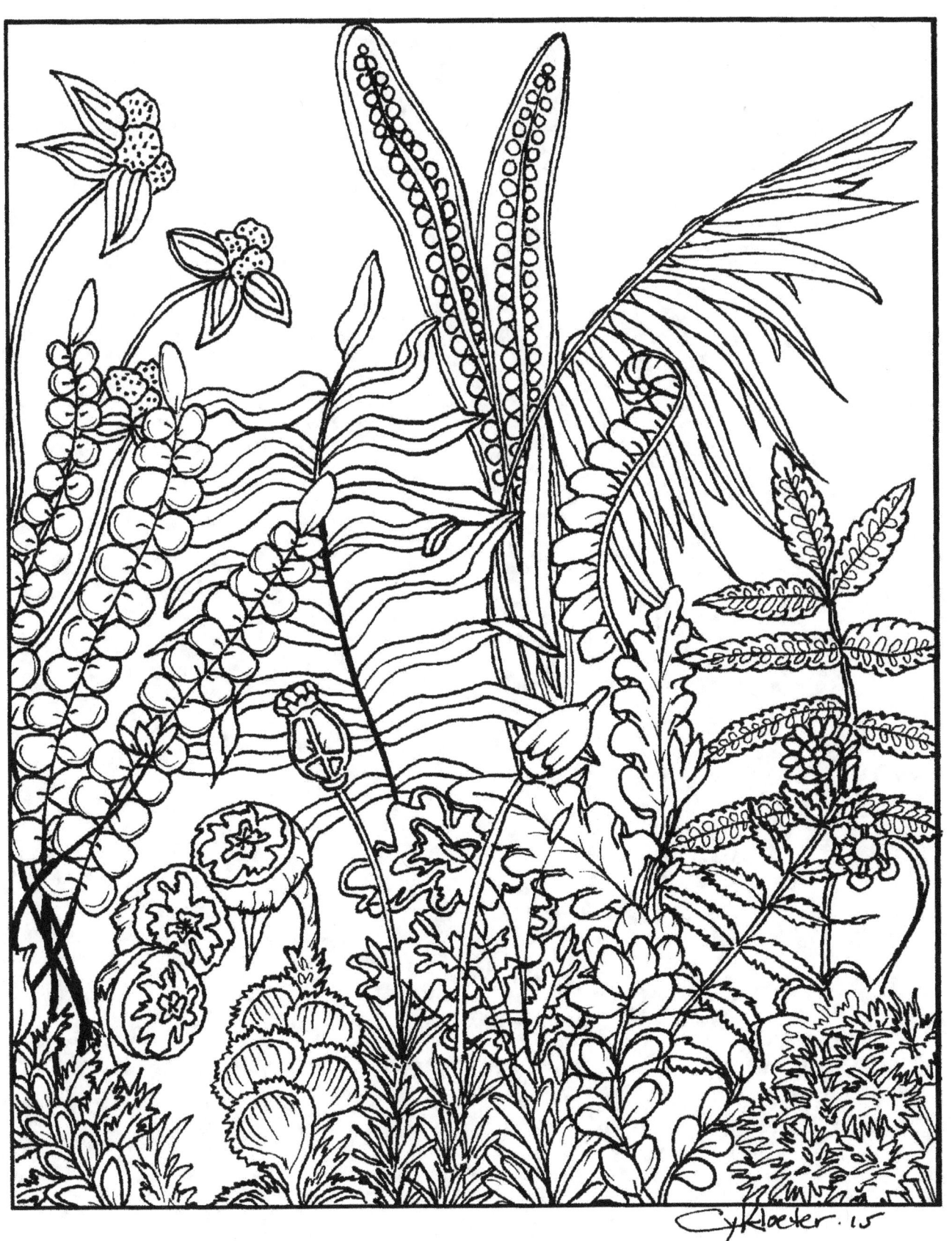

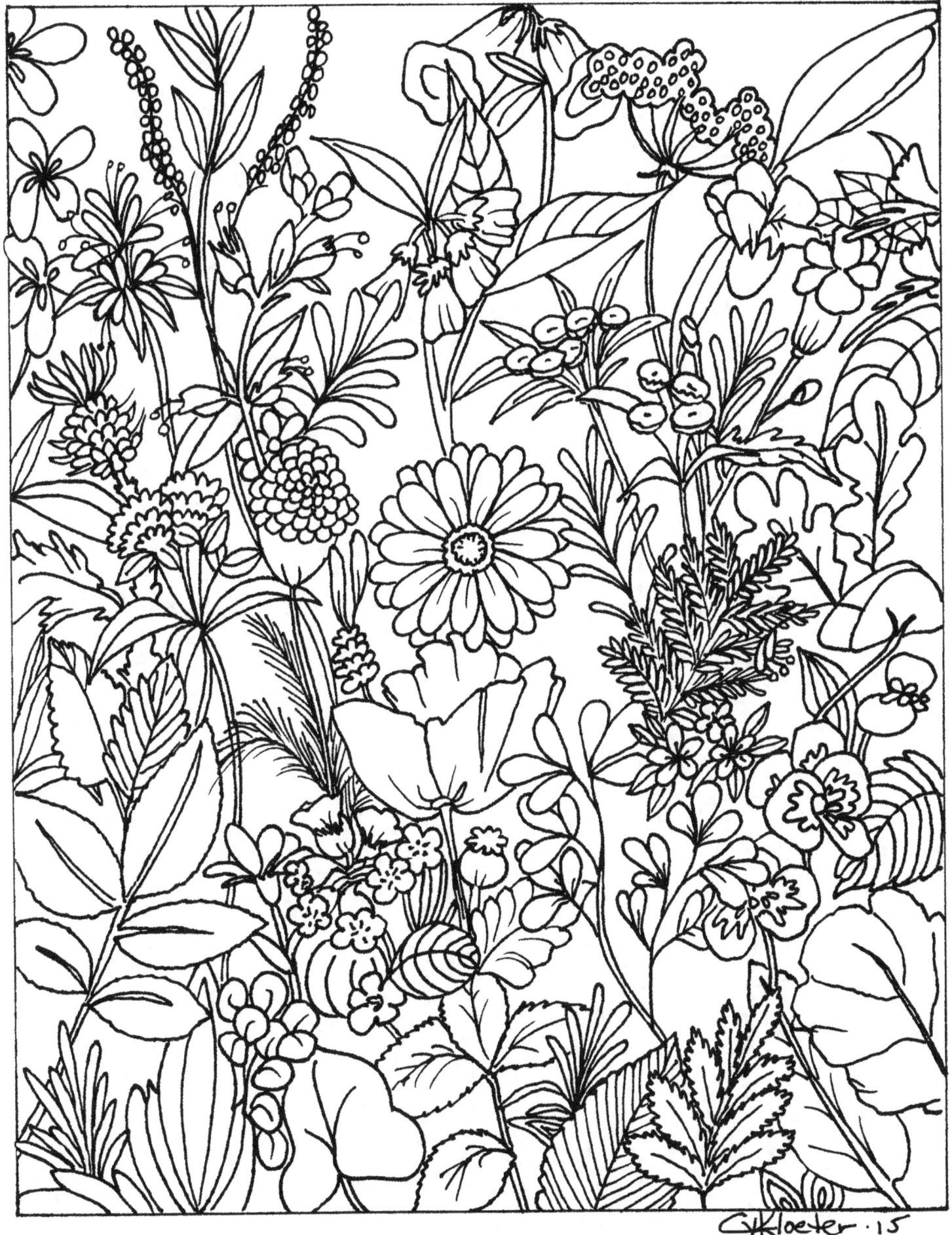

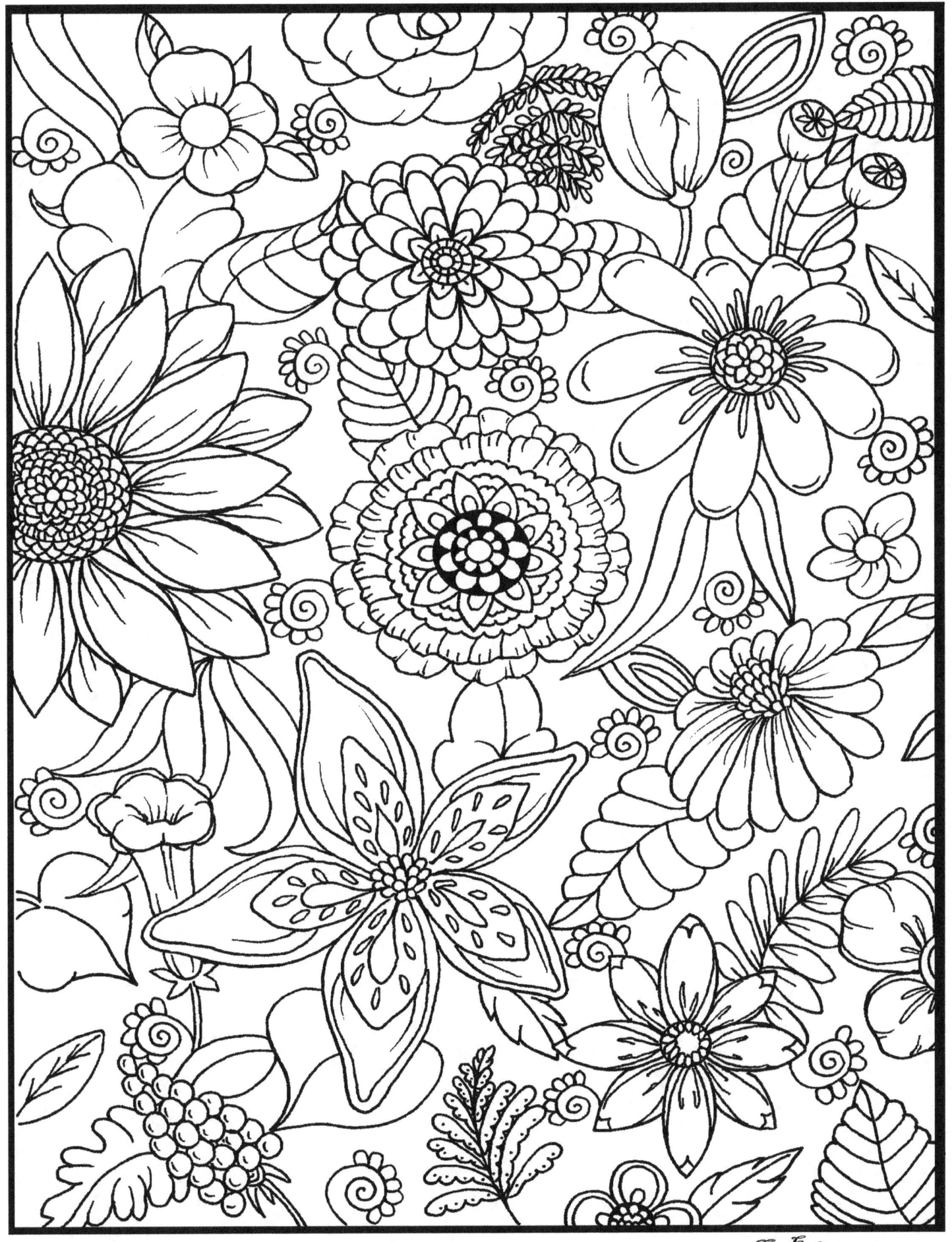

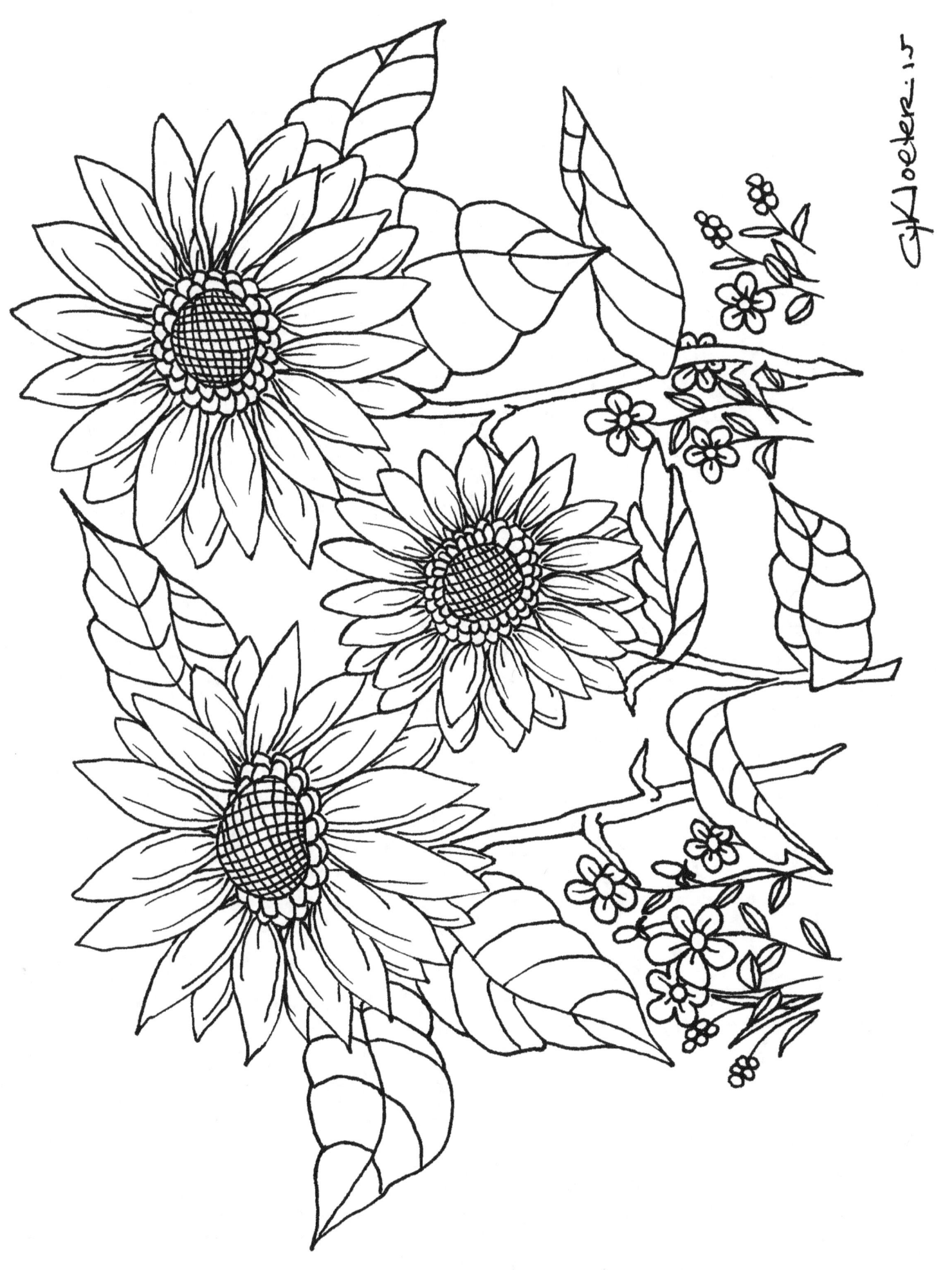

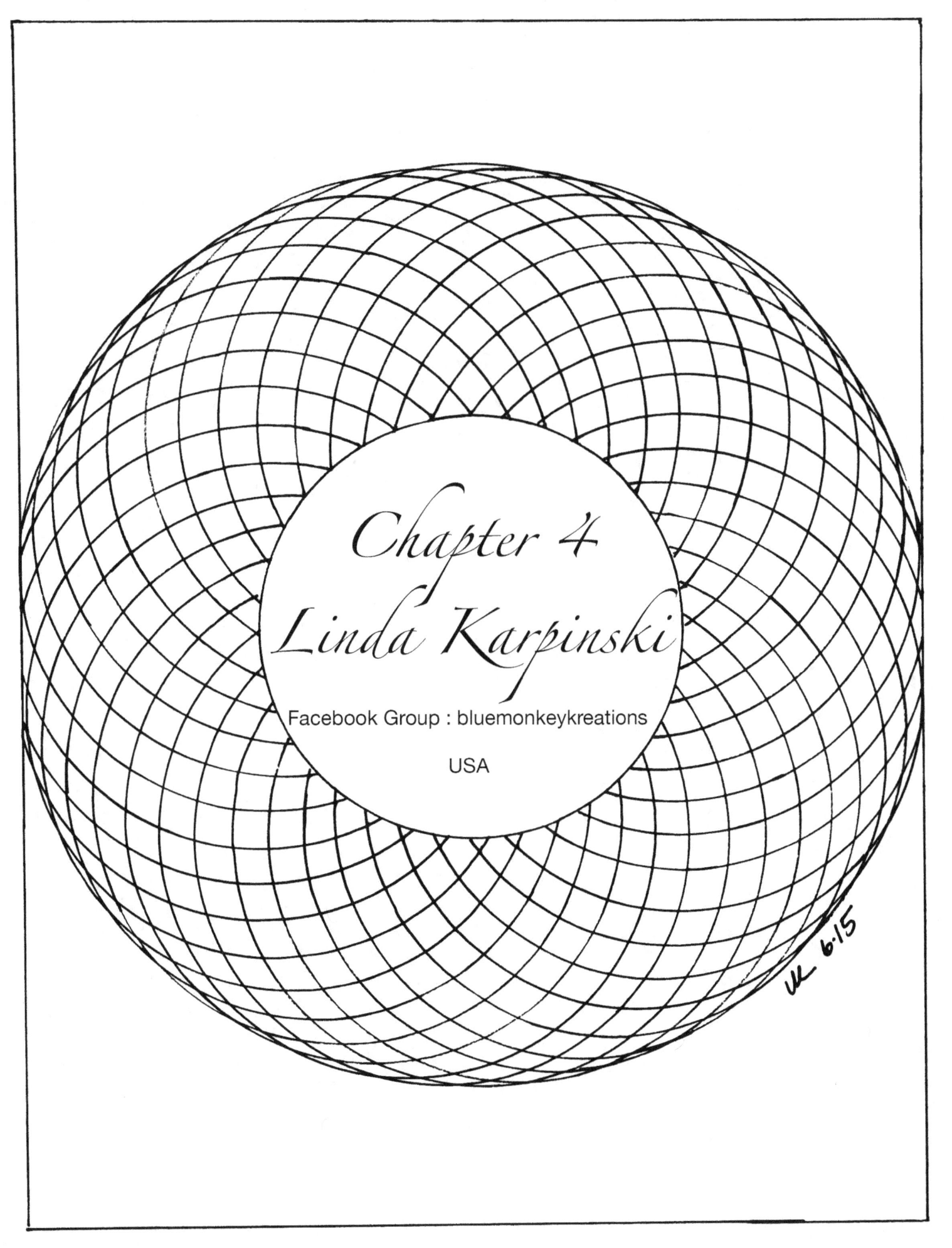

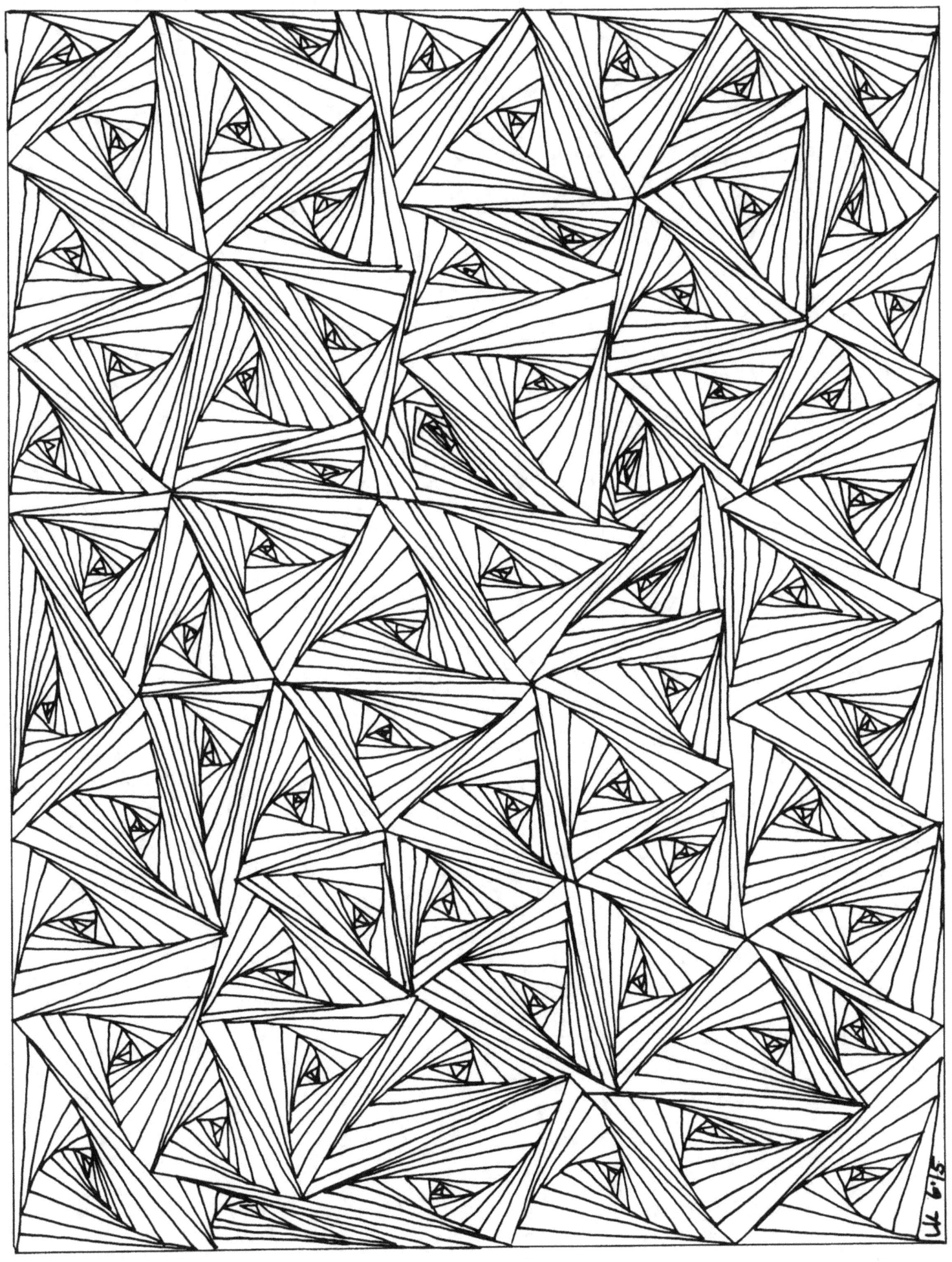

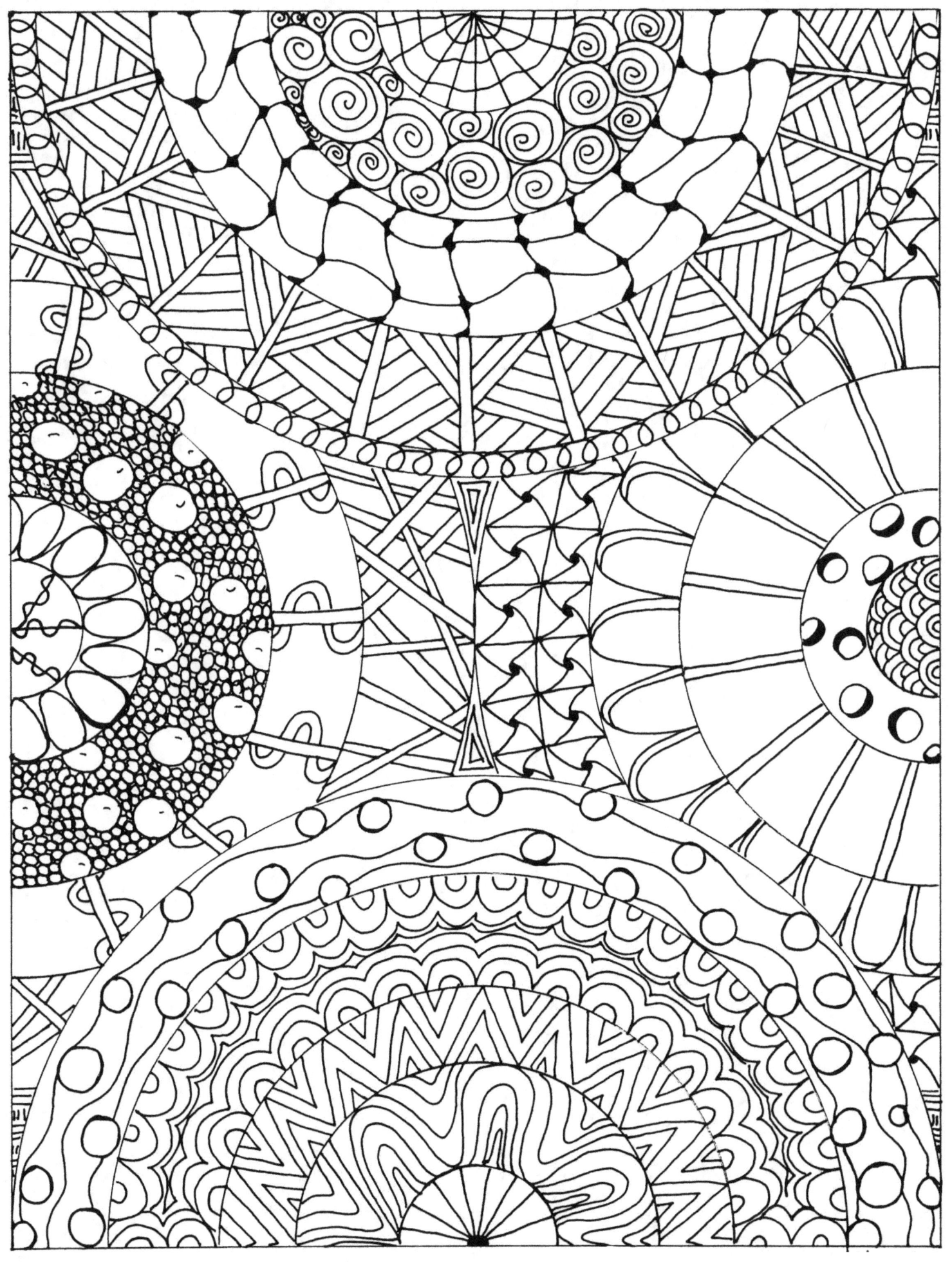

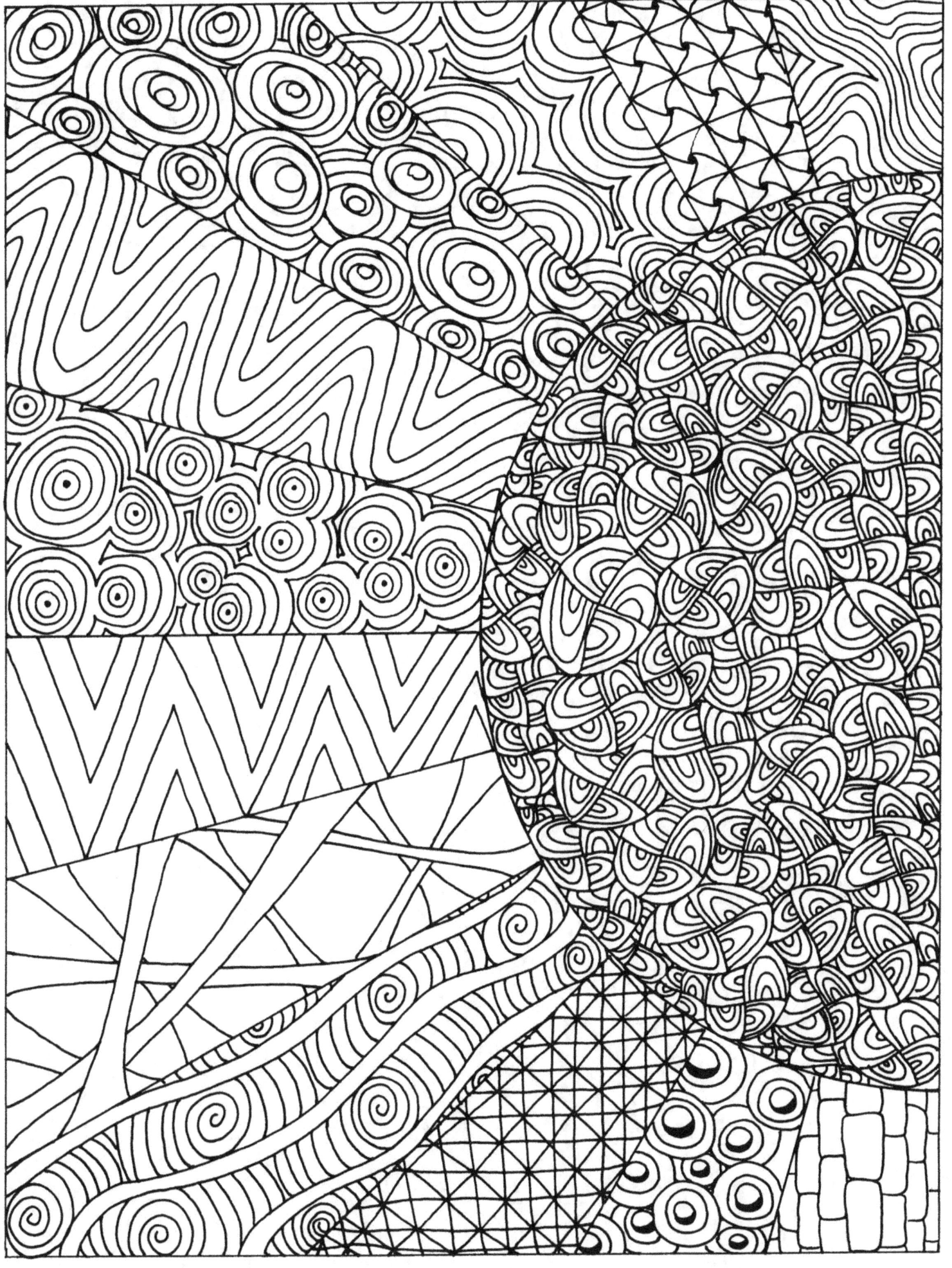

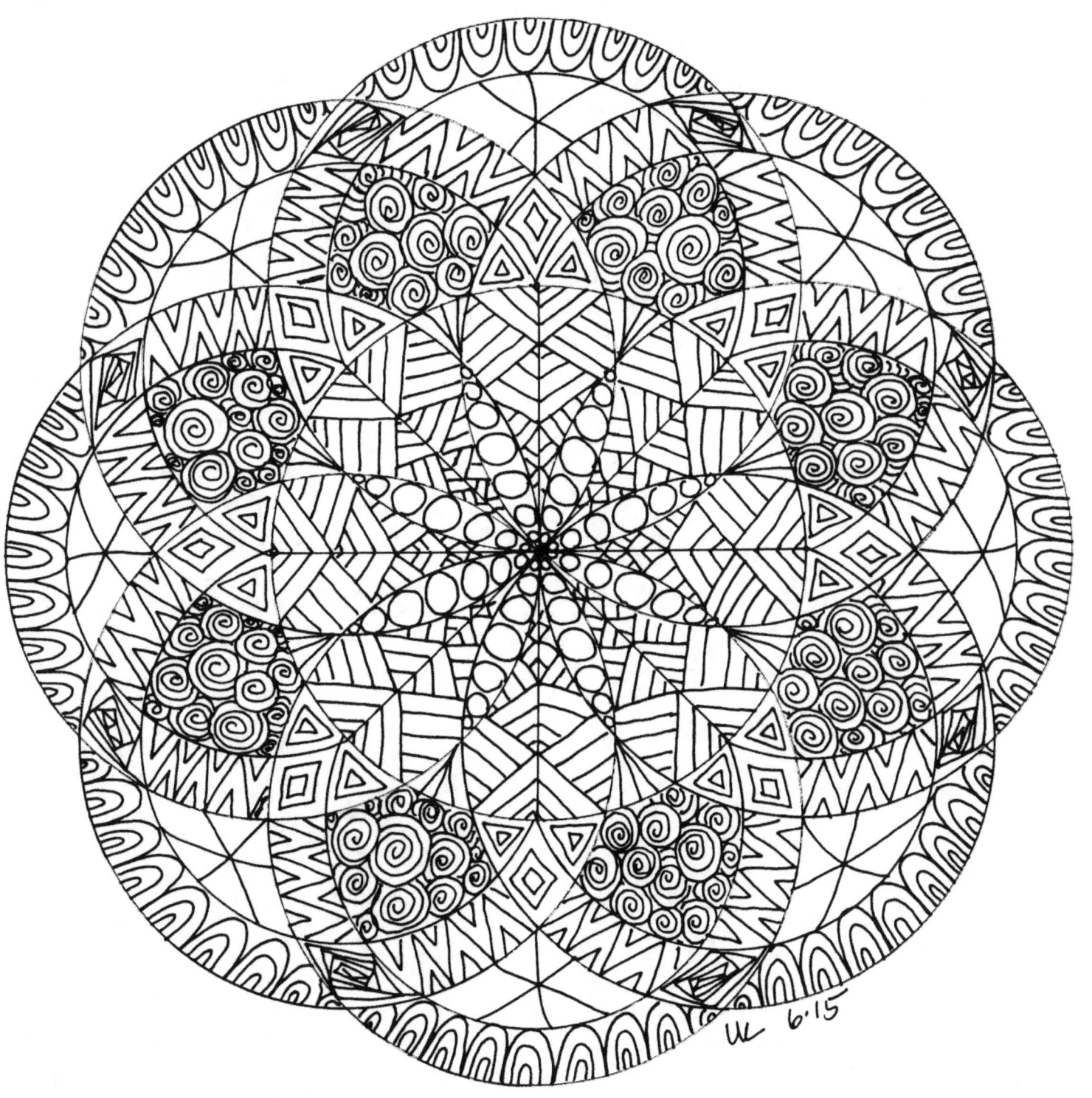

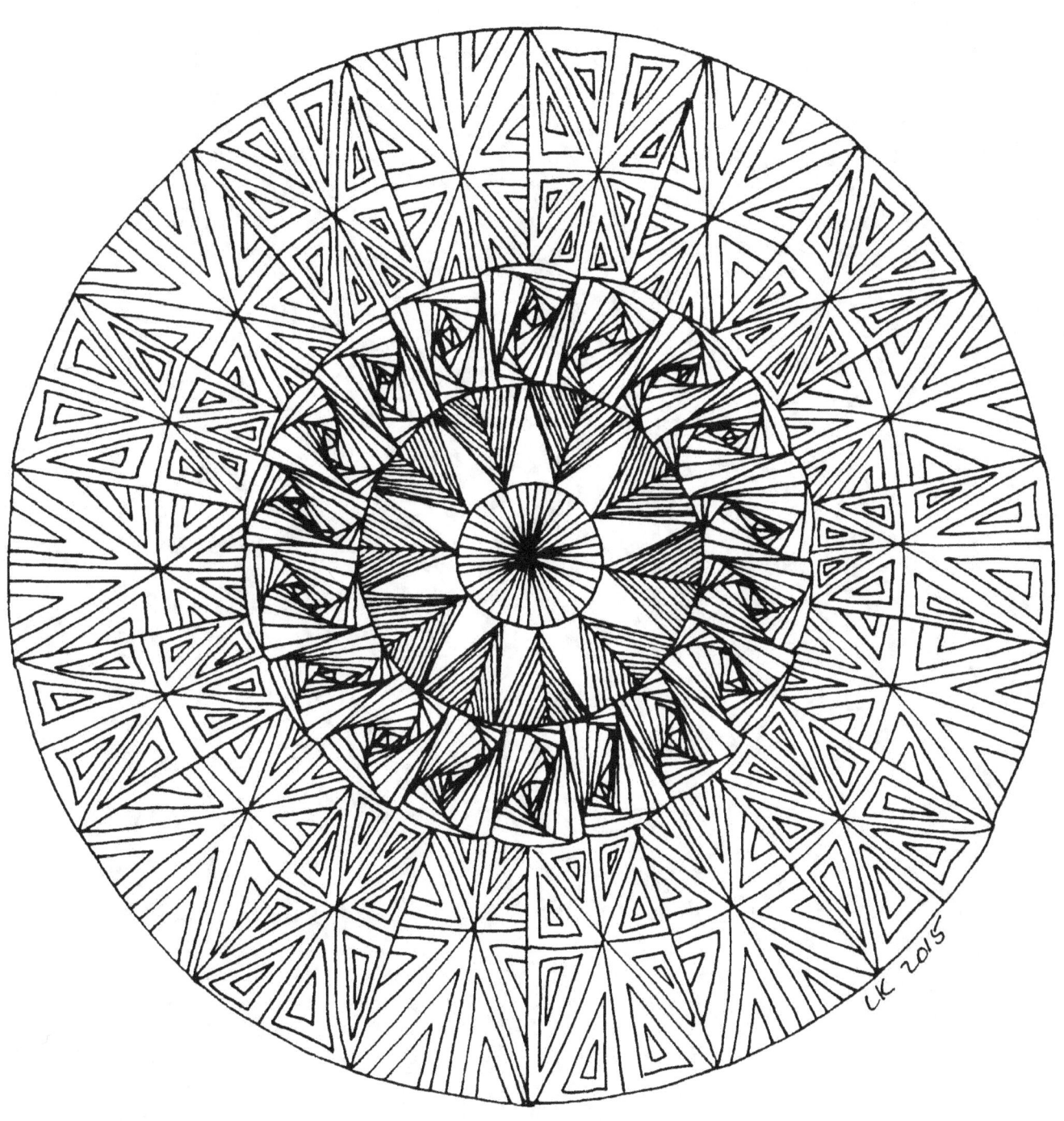

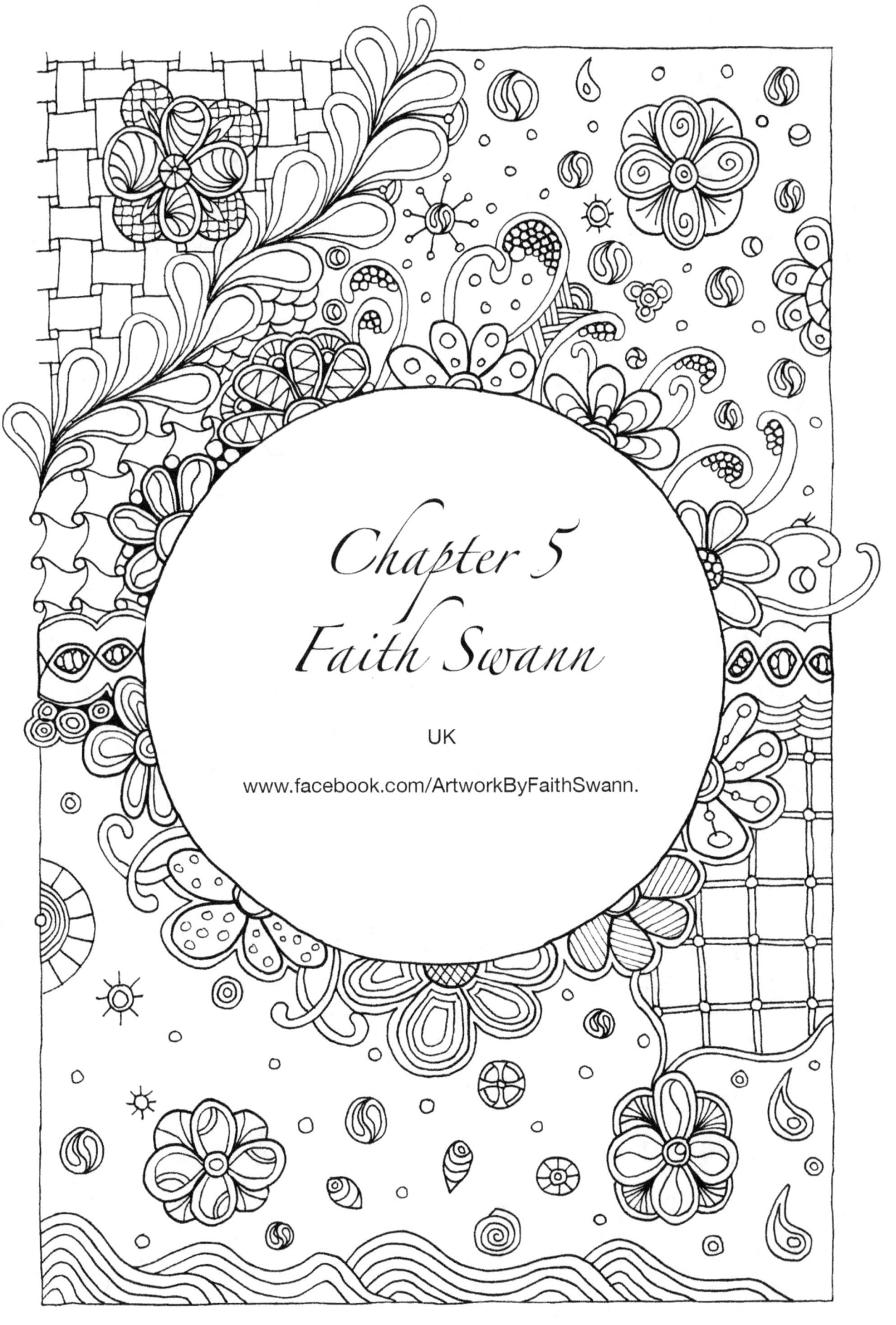

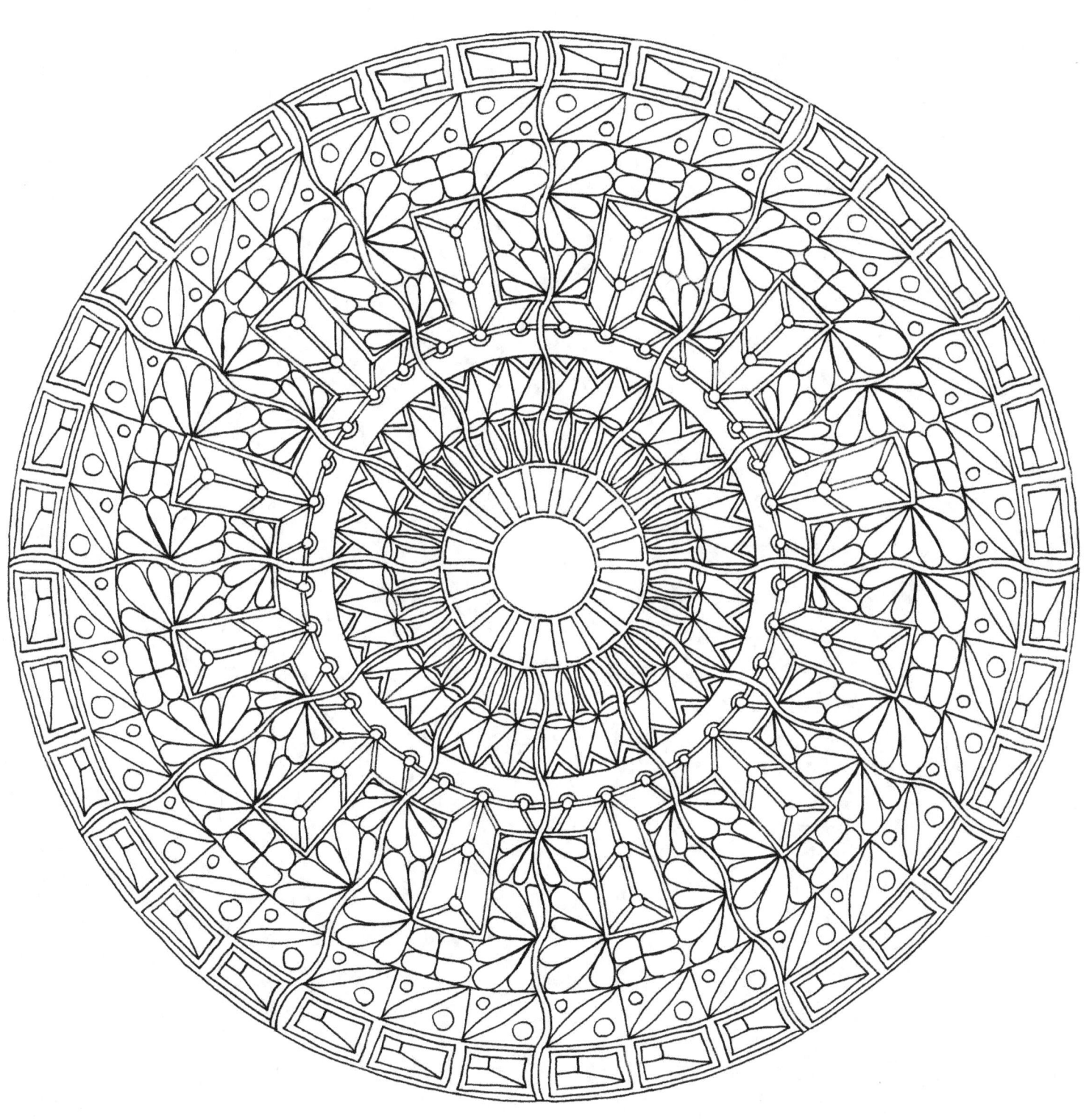

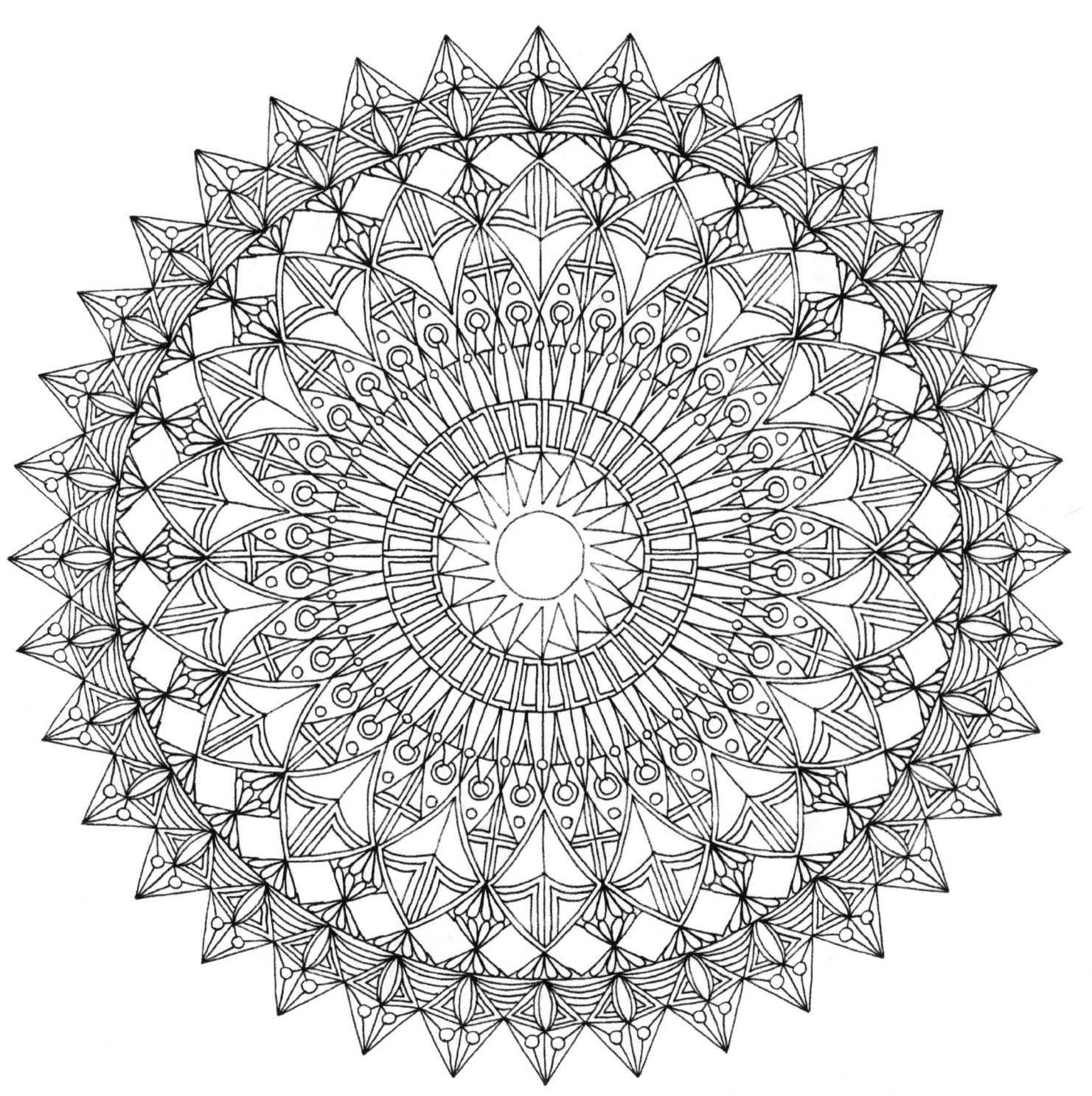

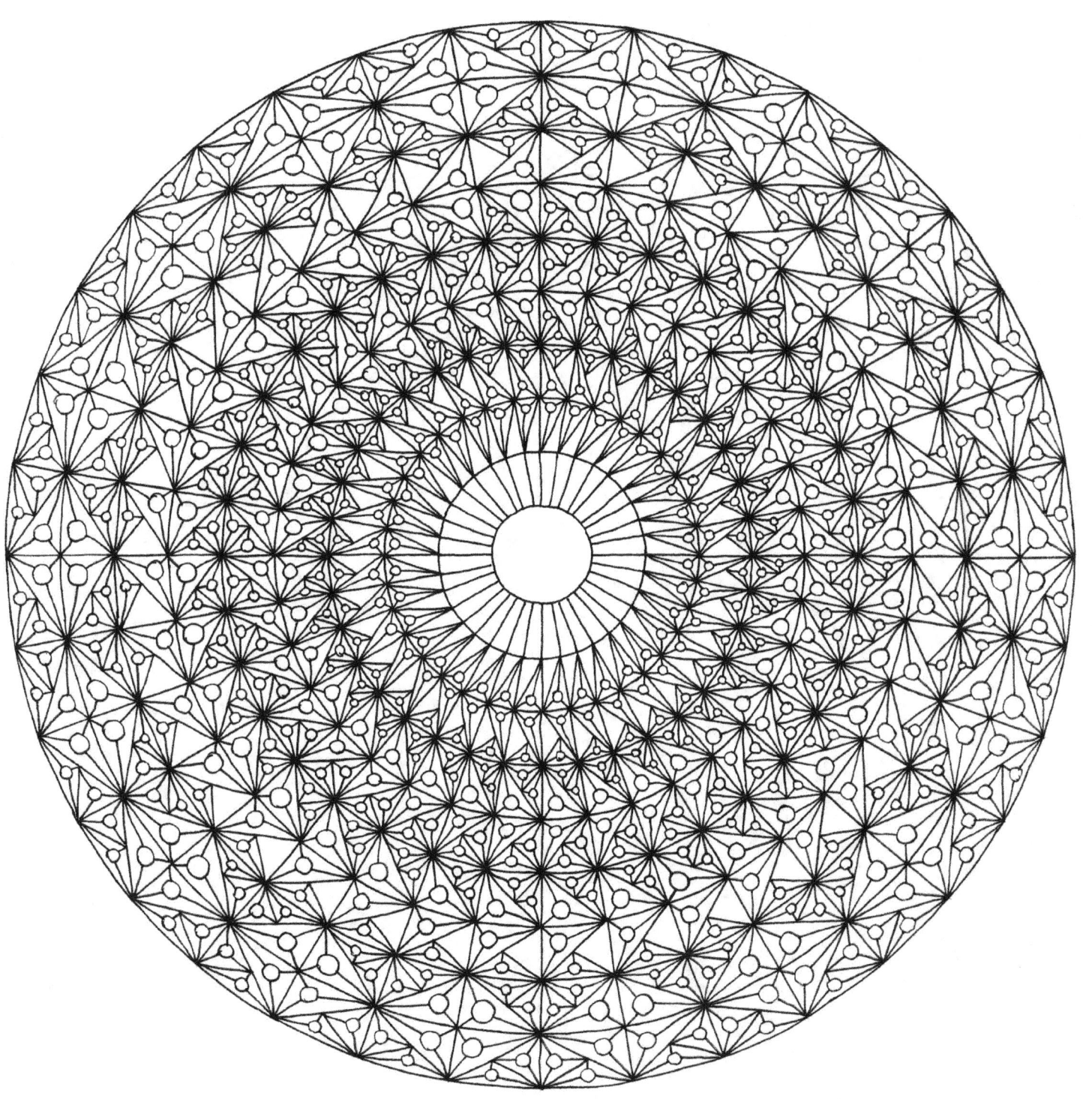

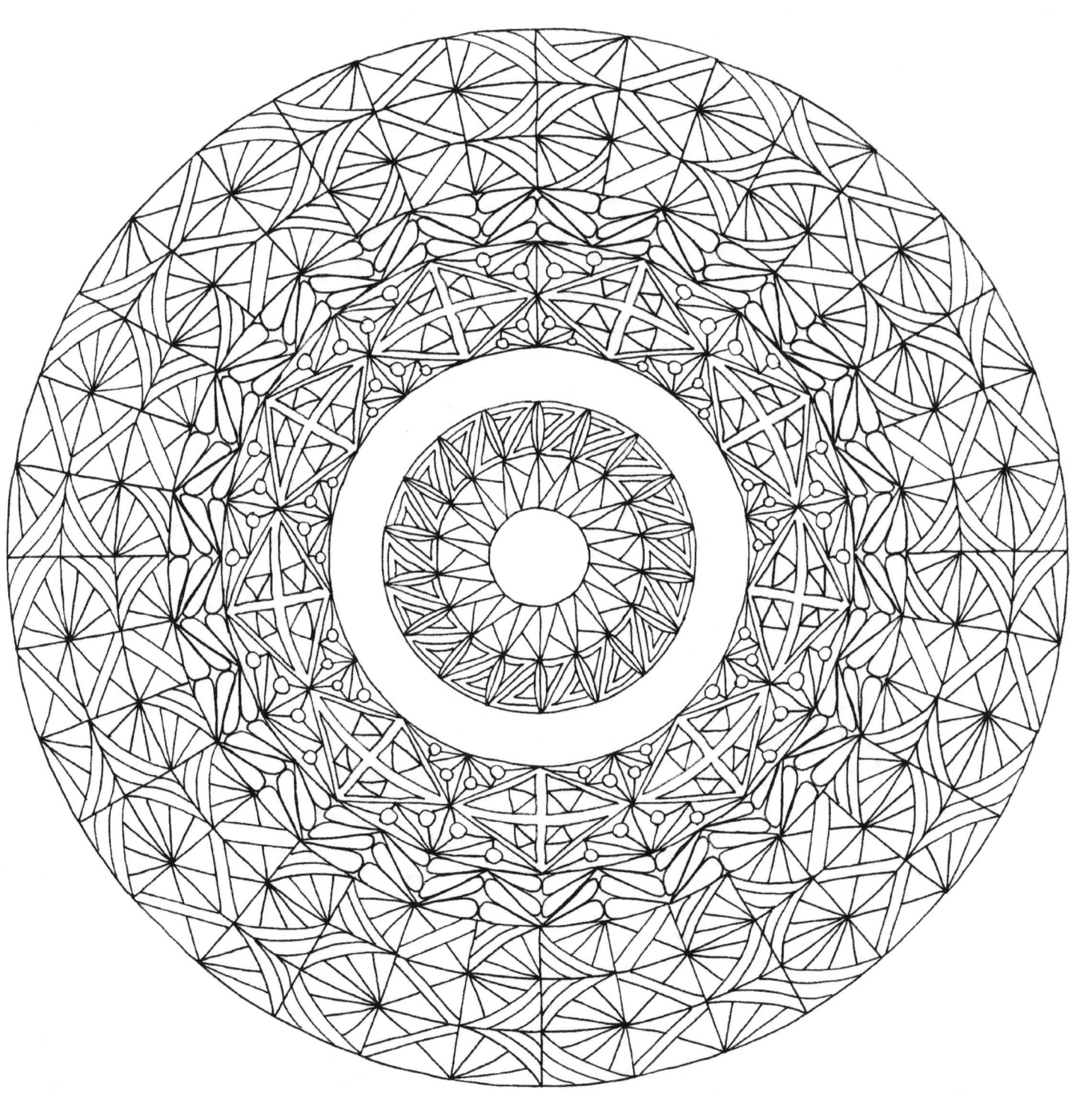

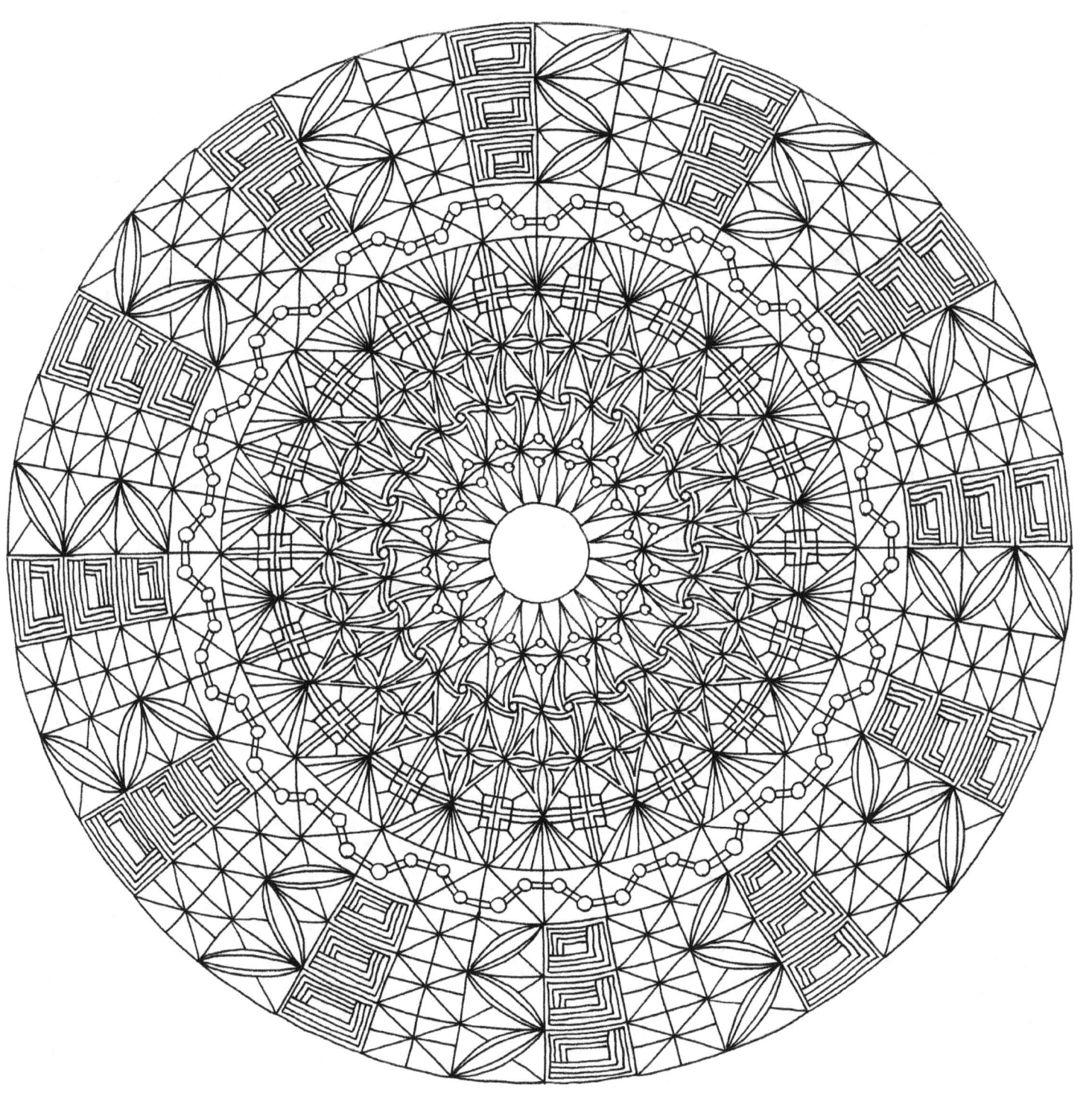

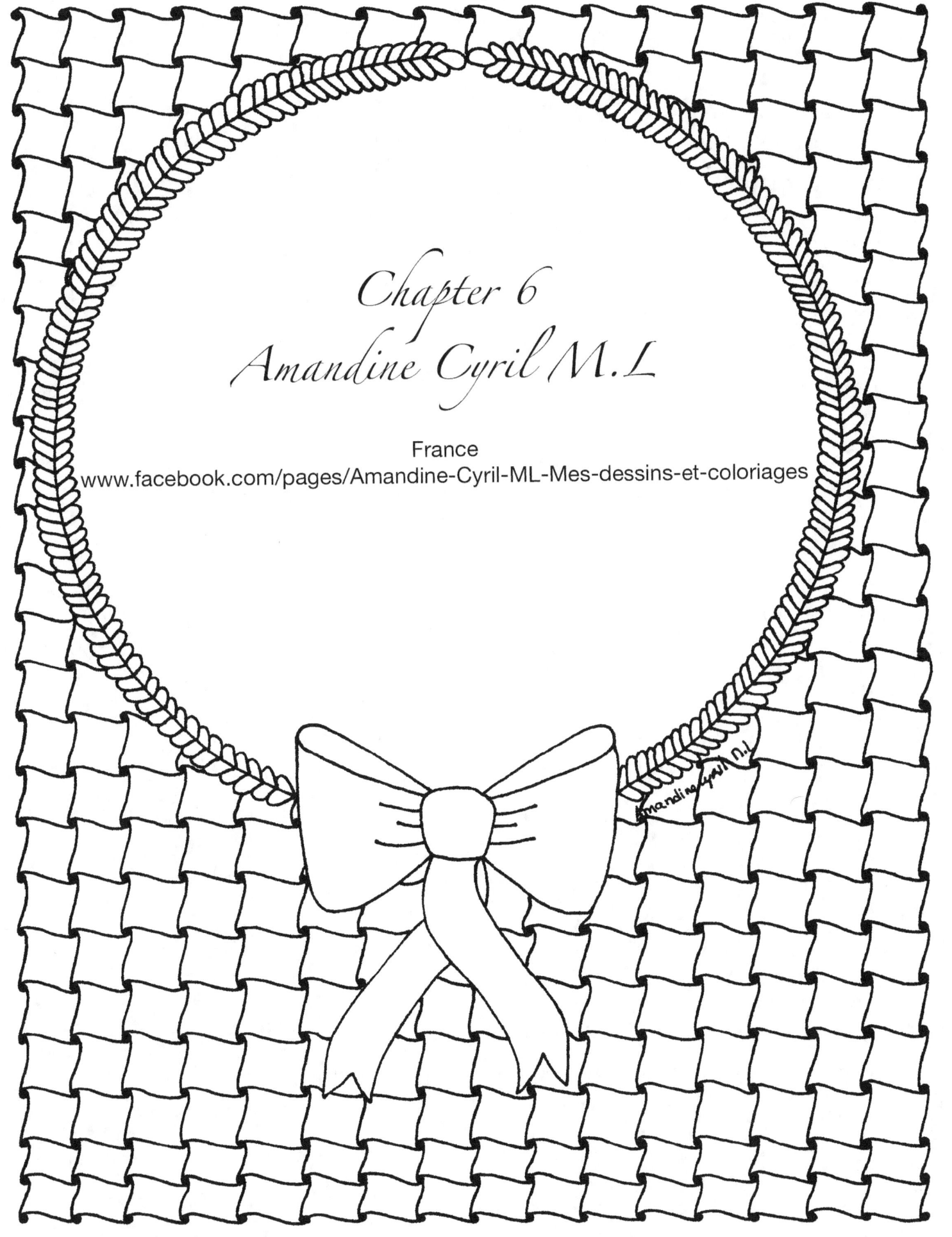

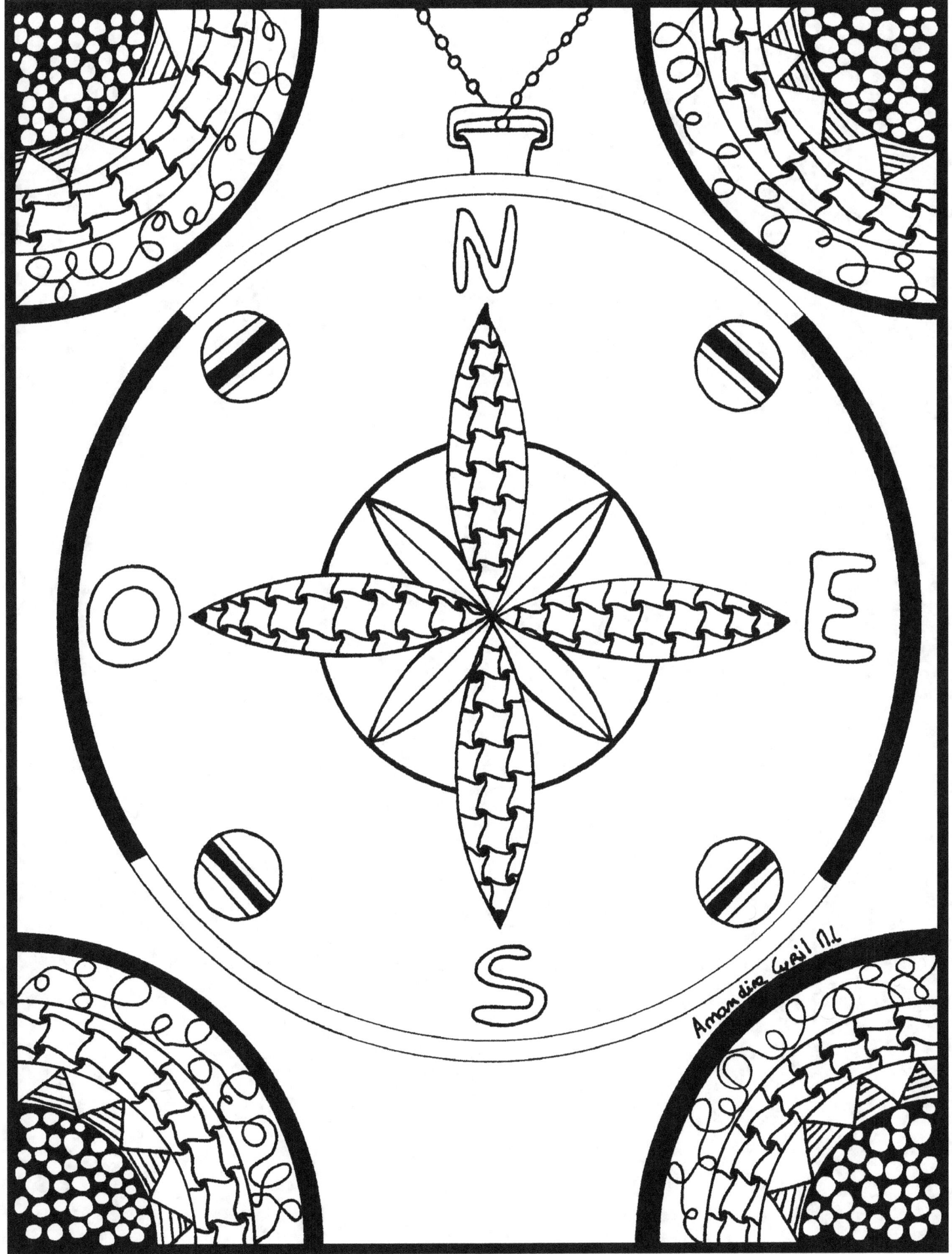

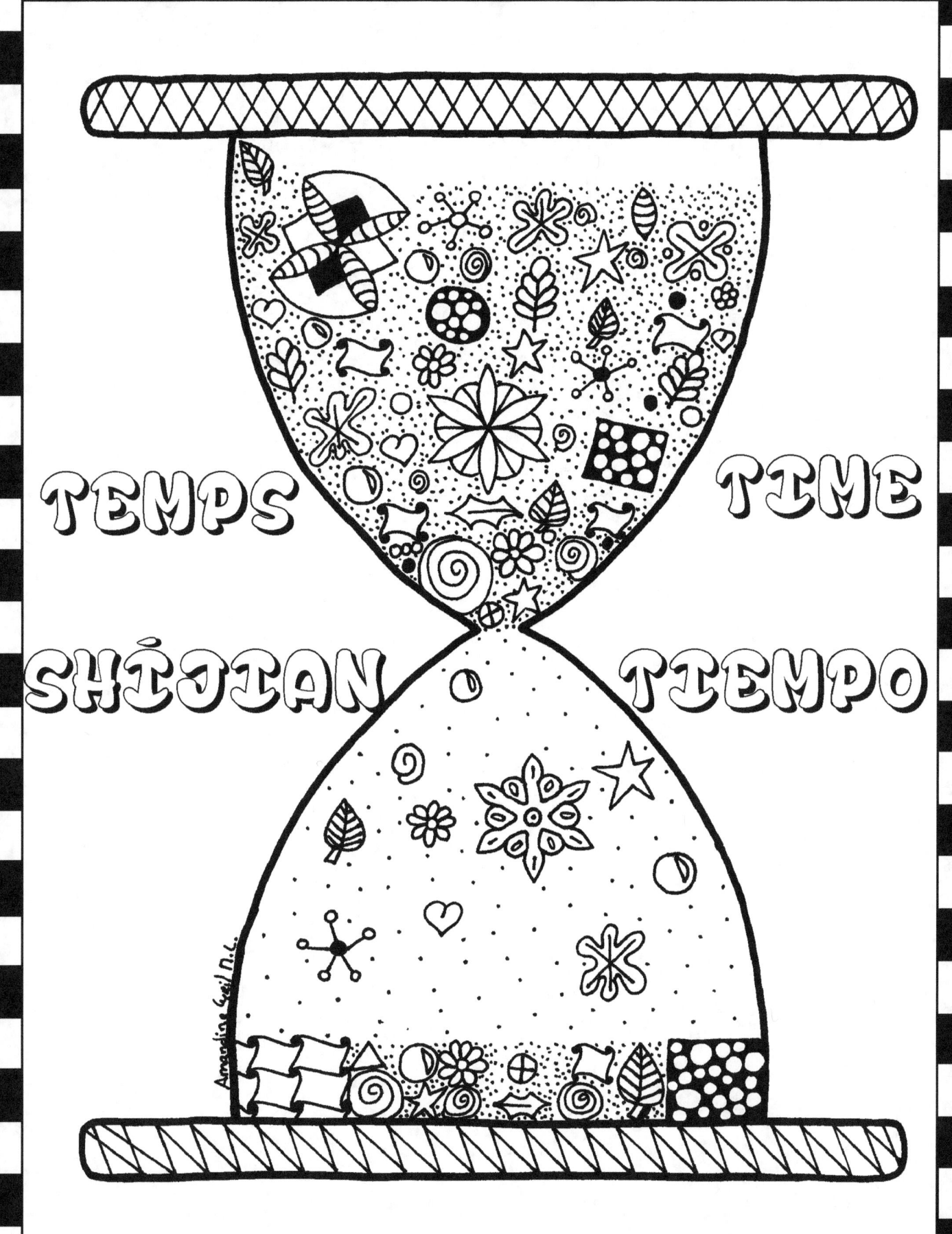

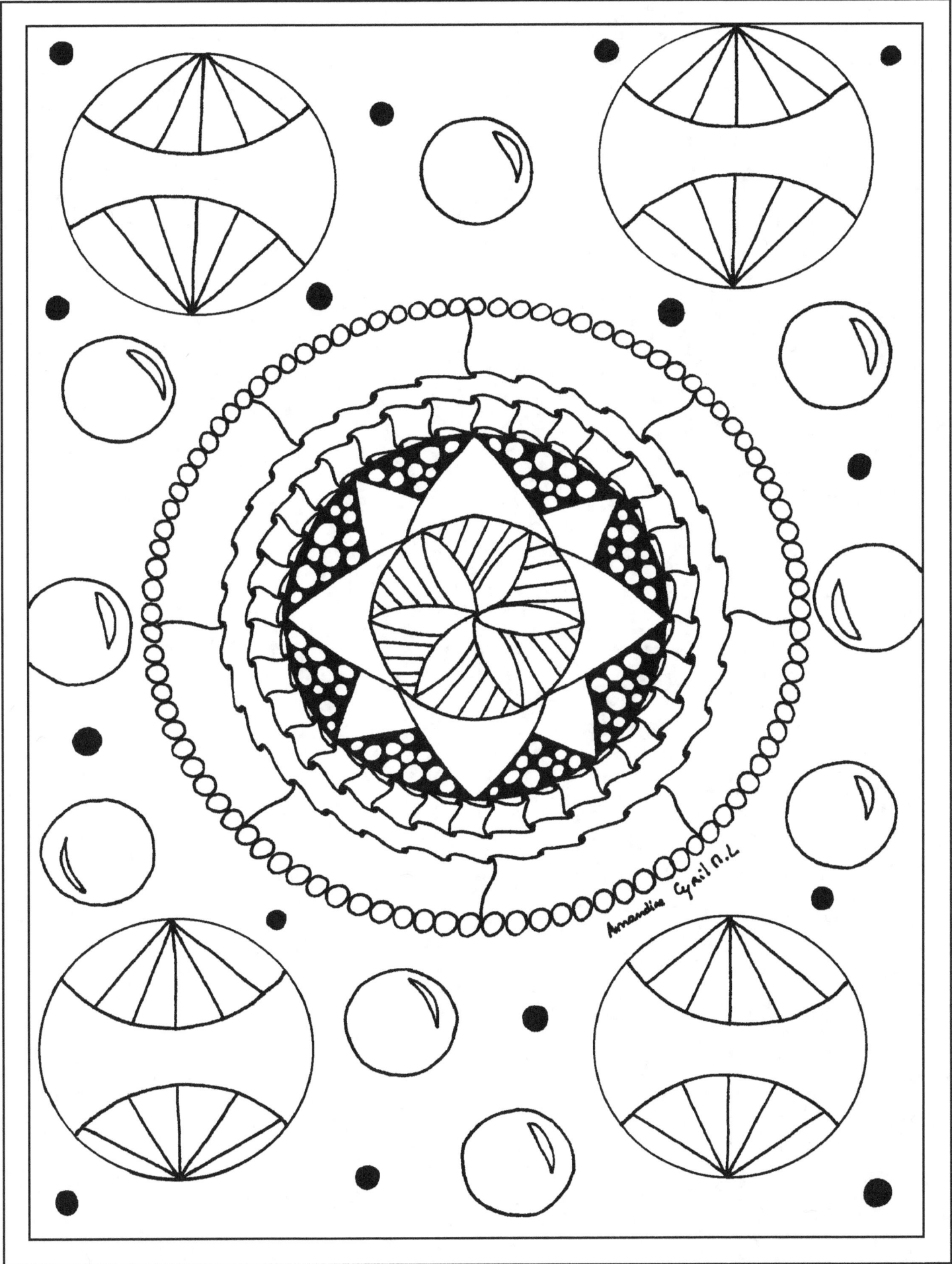

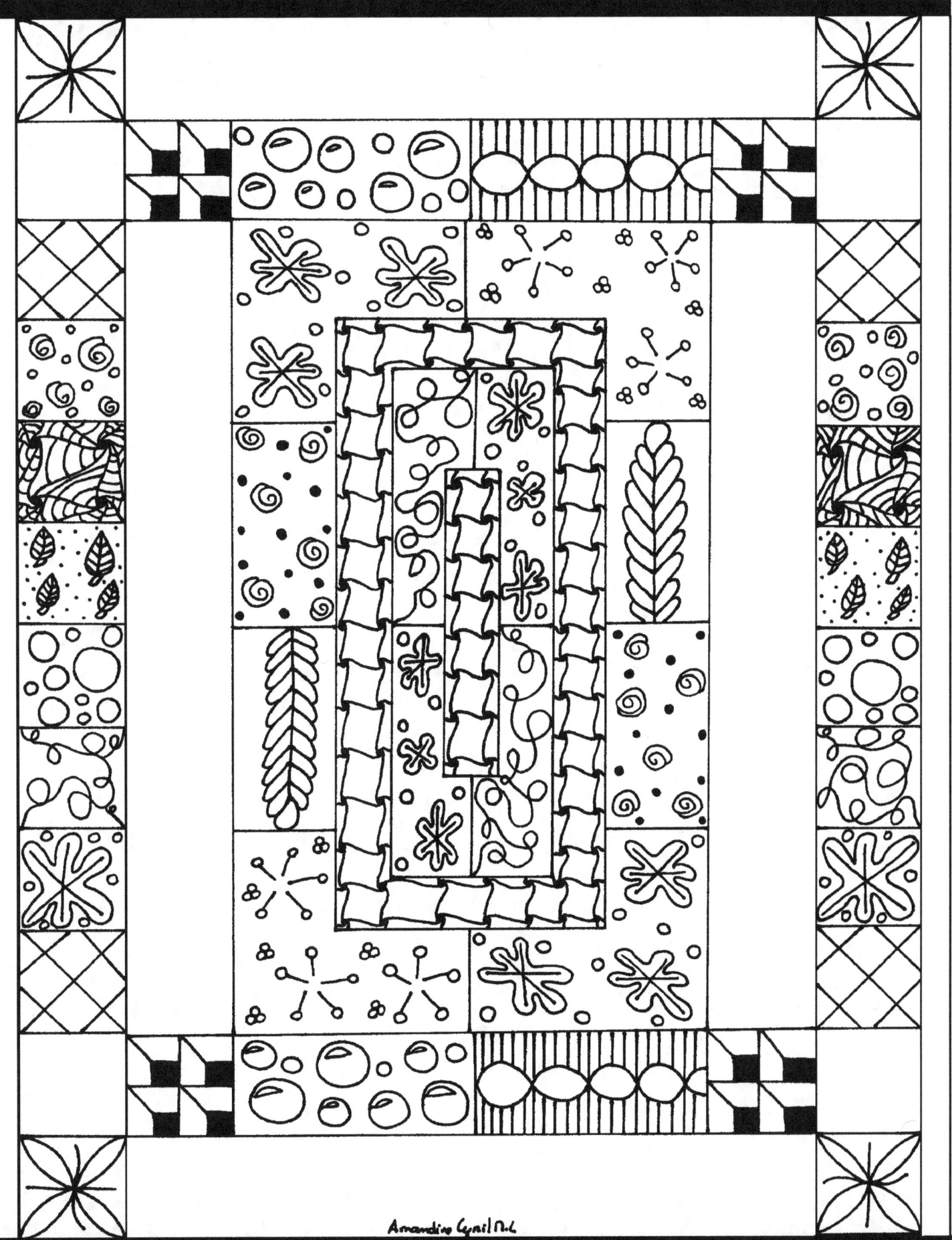

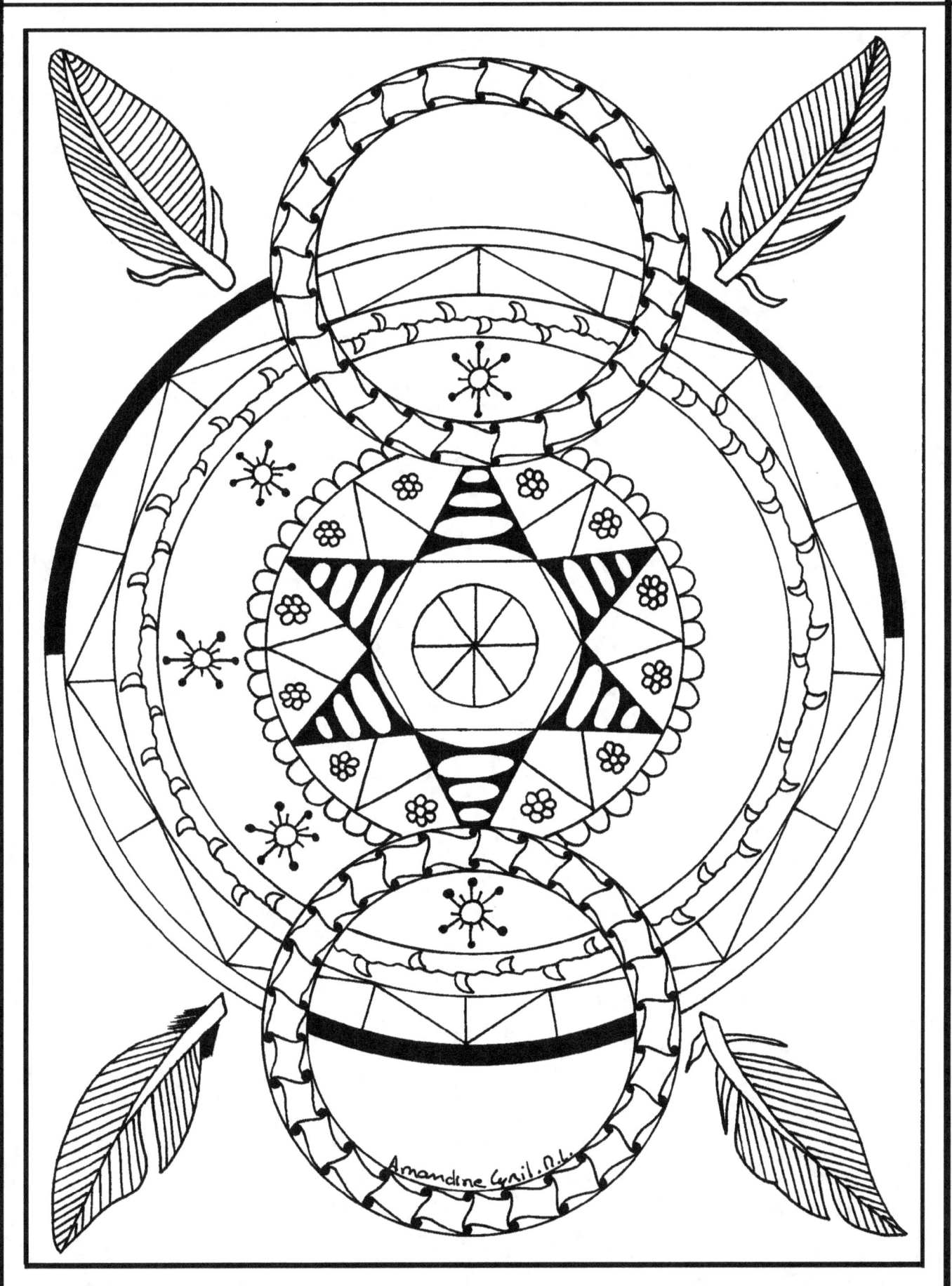

Chapter 7
Mr. End

Mr.End
Horoscope

www.facebook.com/GeometryFlow

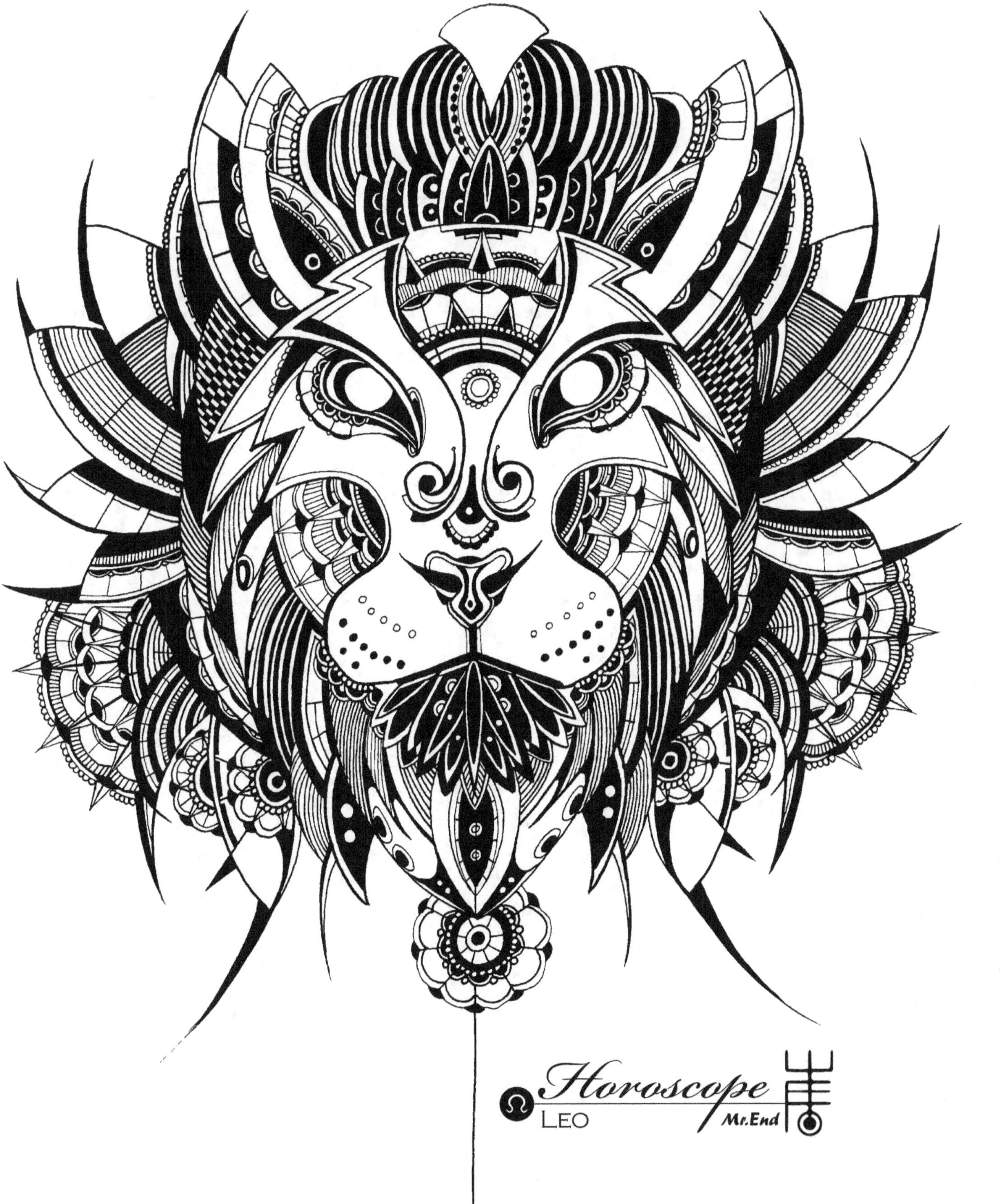

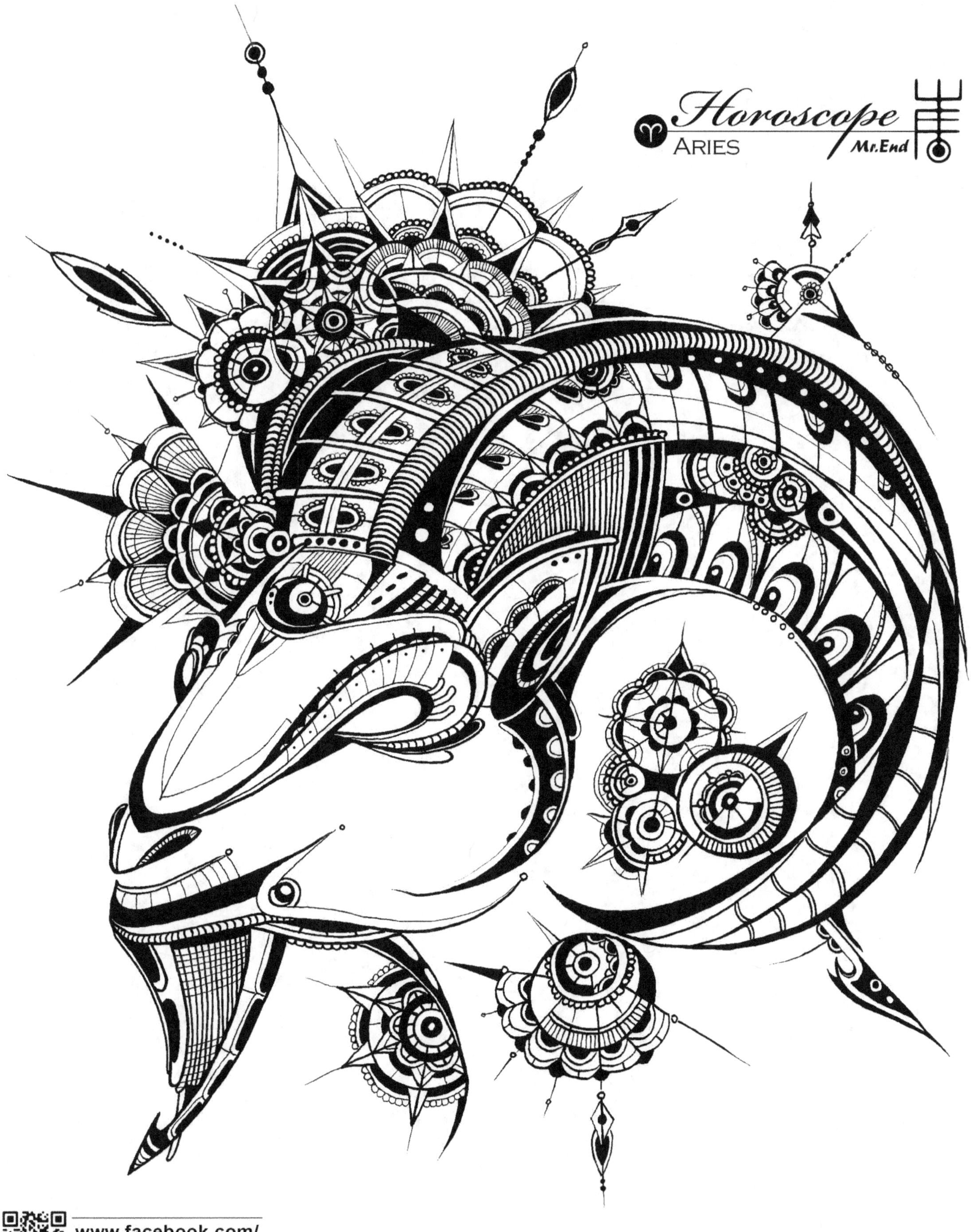

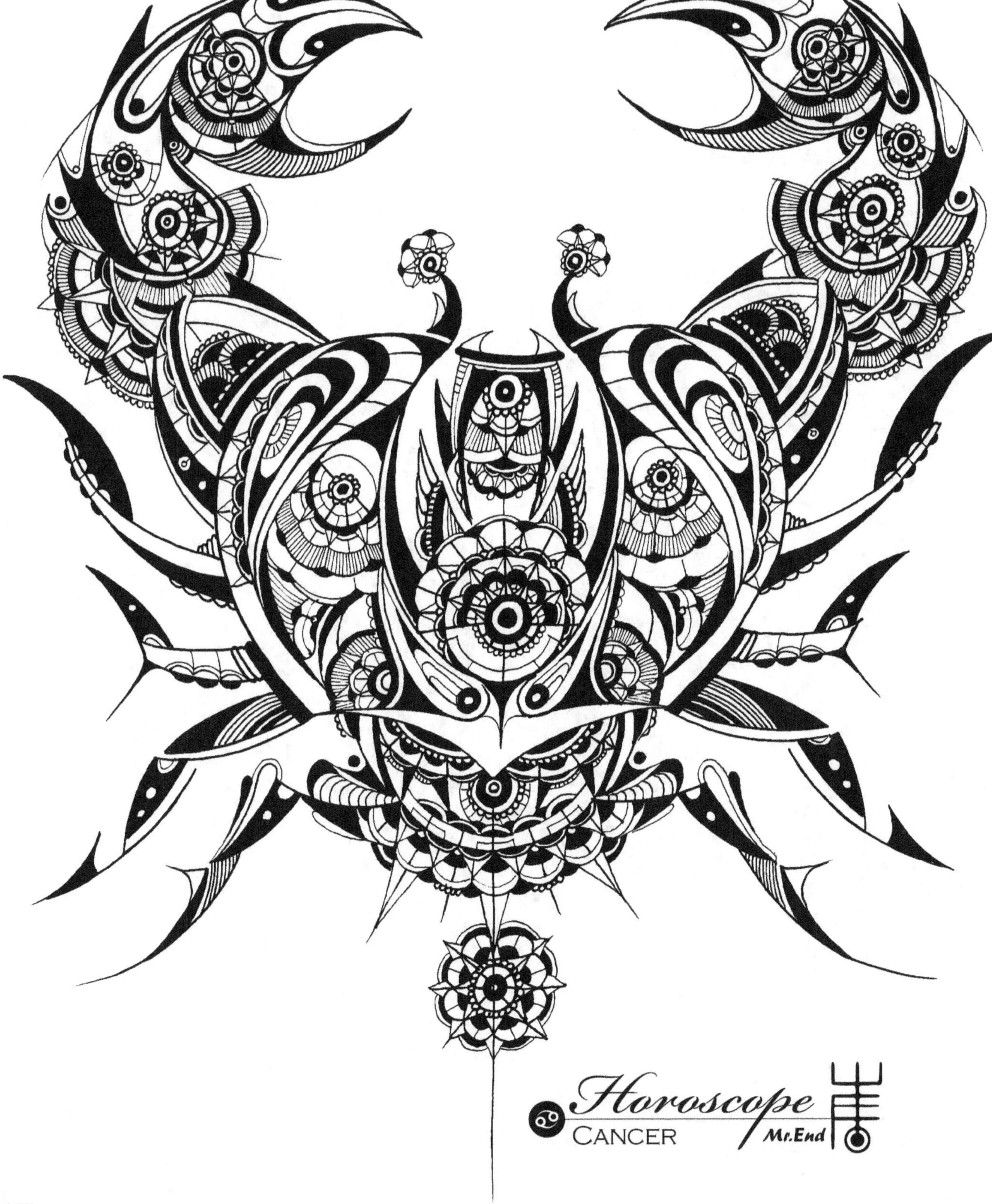

www.facebook.com/
GeometryFlow

Horoscope CANCER — Mr.End

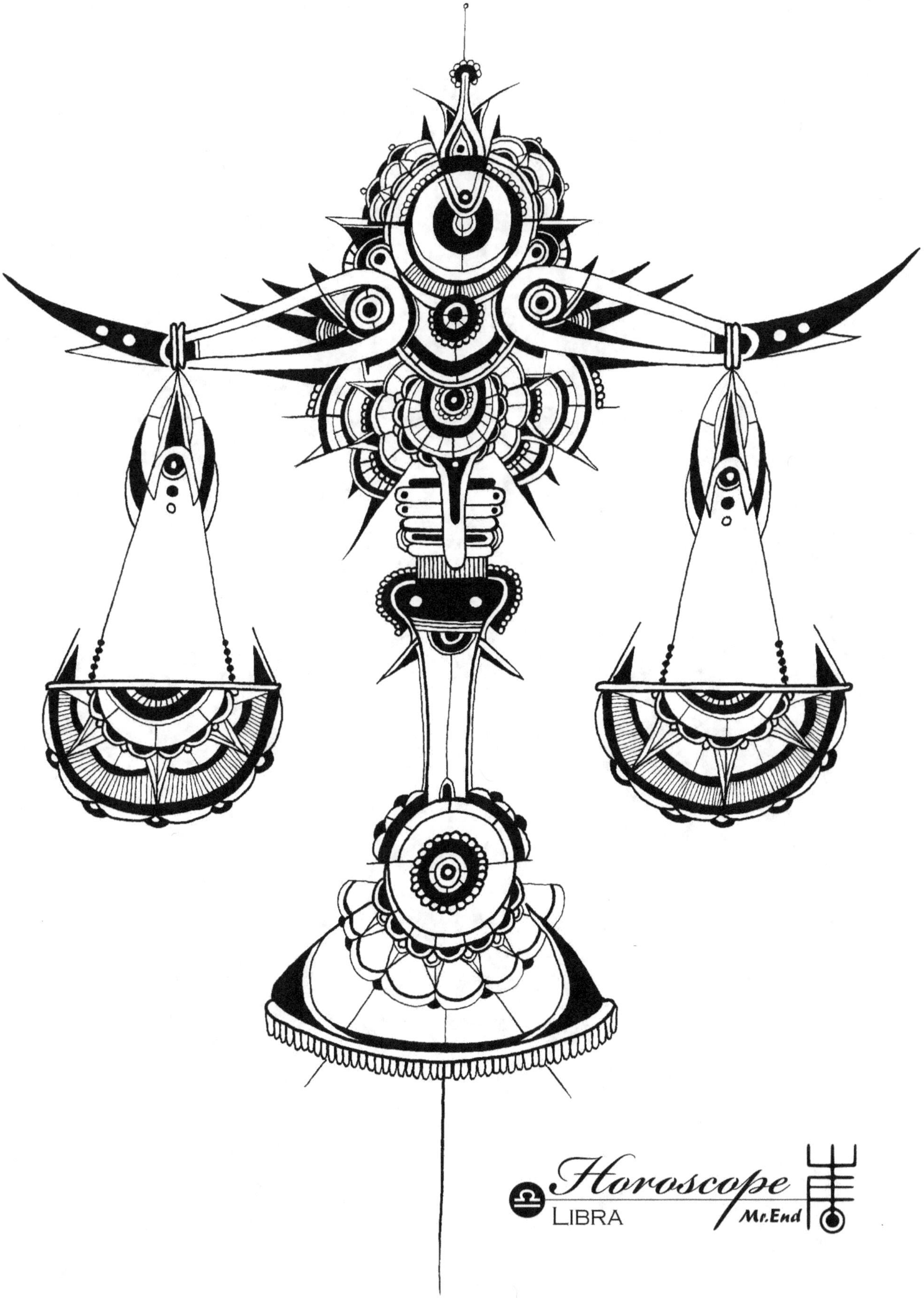

Horoscope
LIBRA Mr.End

www.facebook.com/
GeometryFlow

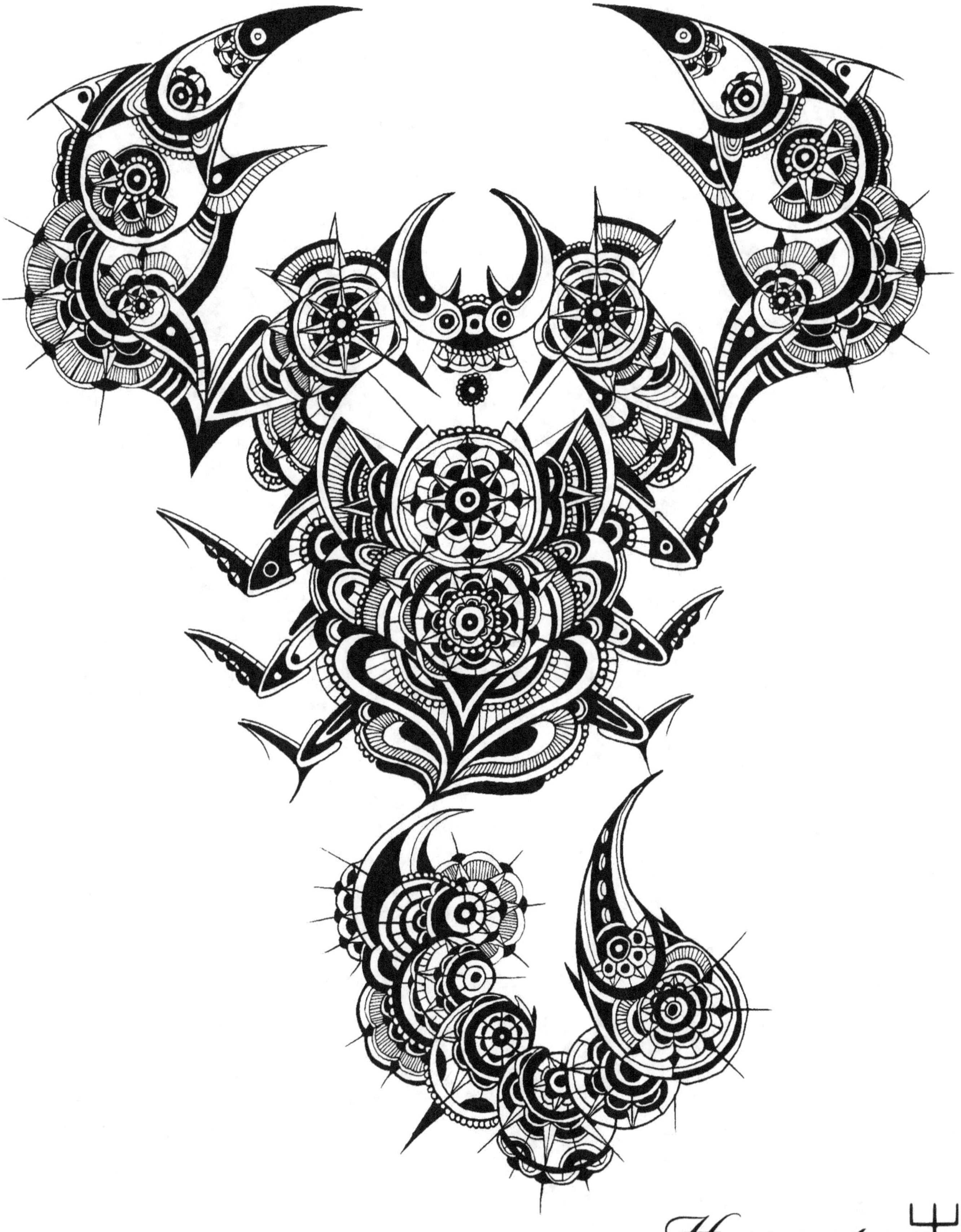

www.facebook.com/GeometryFlow

Horoscope
SCORPIO
Mr.End

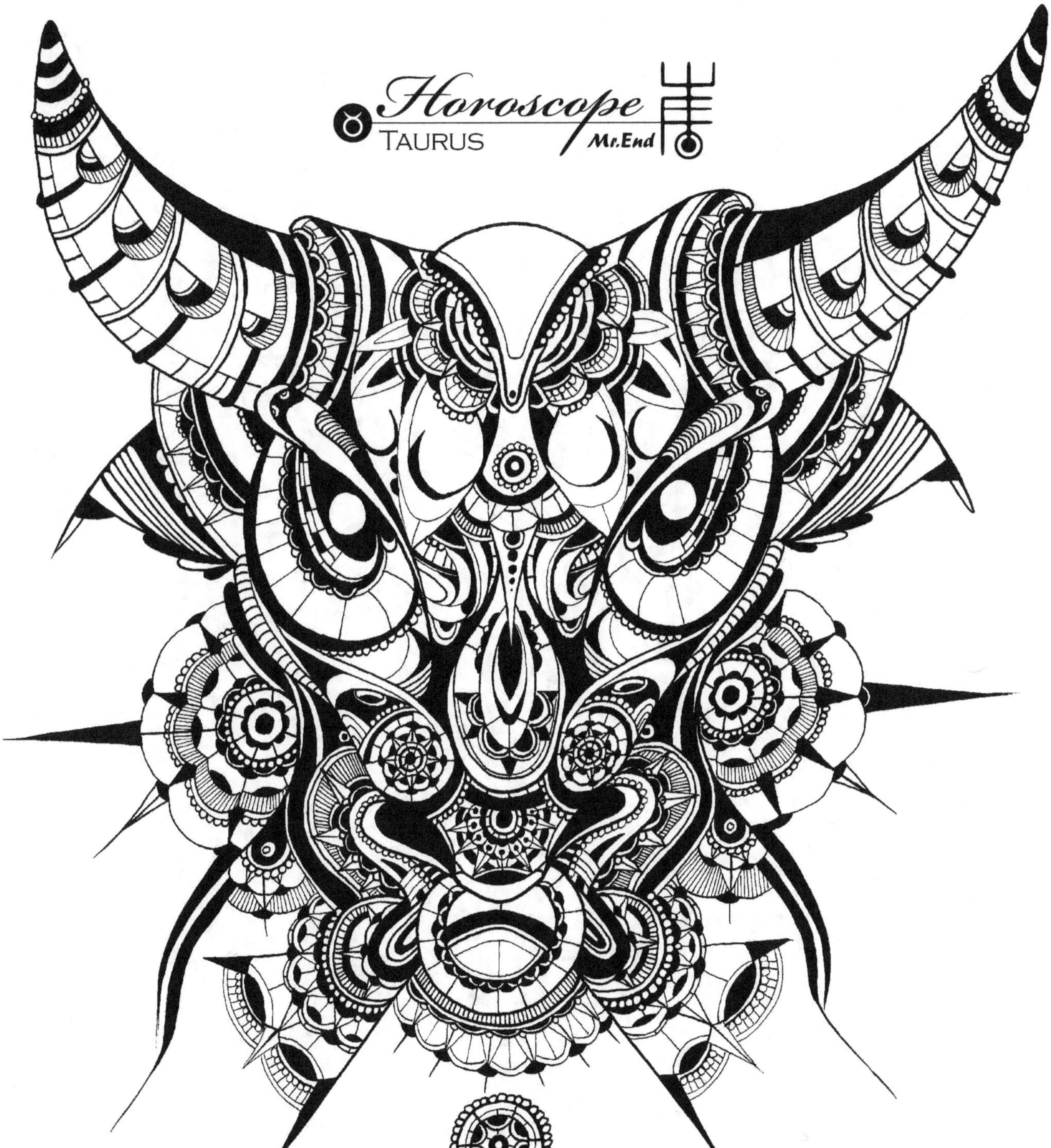

Horoscope
TAURUS

www.facebook.com/
GeometryFlow

Chapter 8
Fabienne Tosi

Switzerland
Facebook :Fabienne Tosi

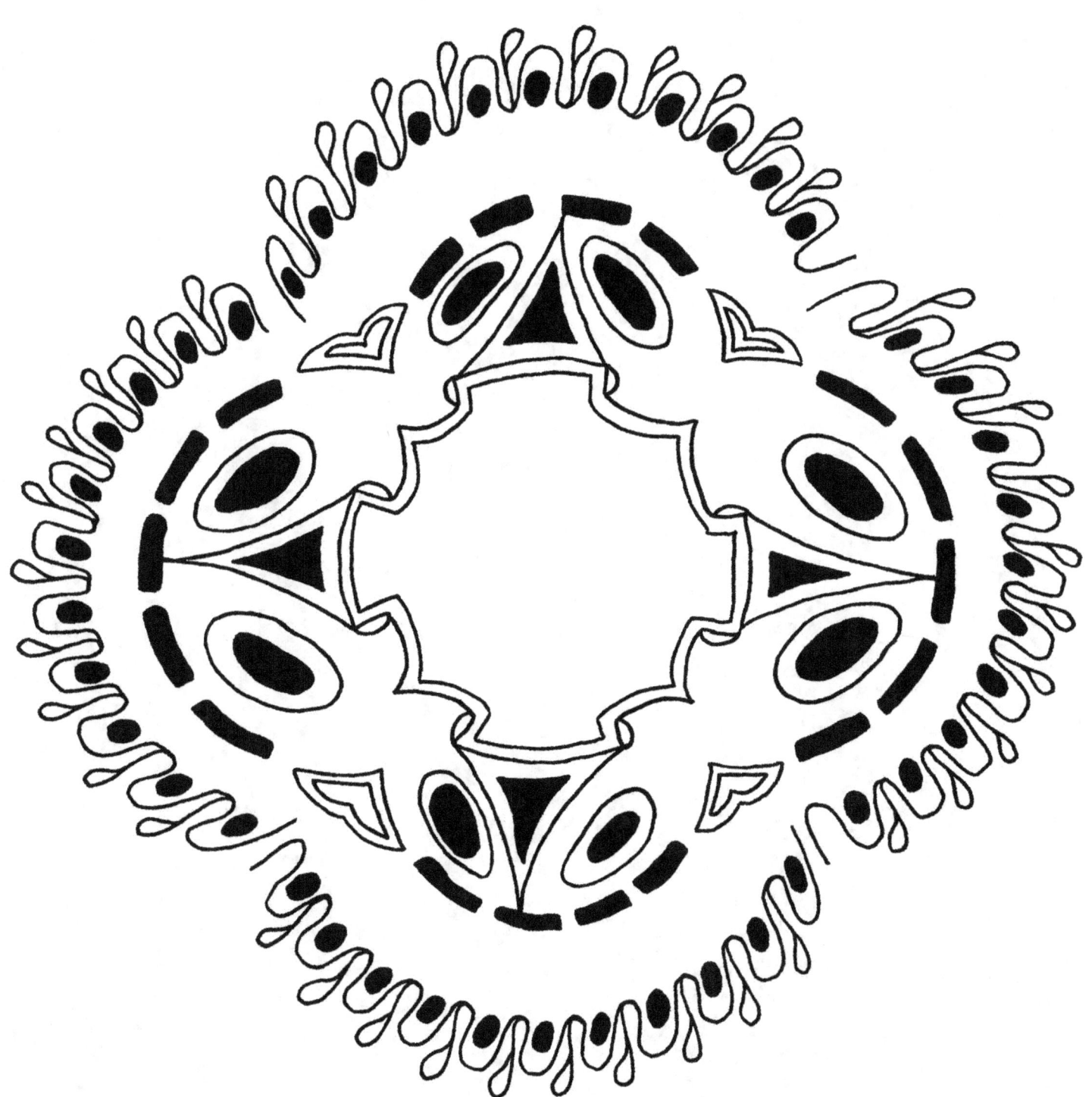

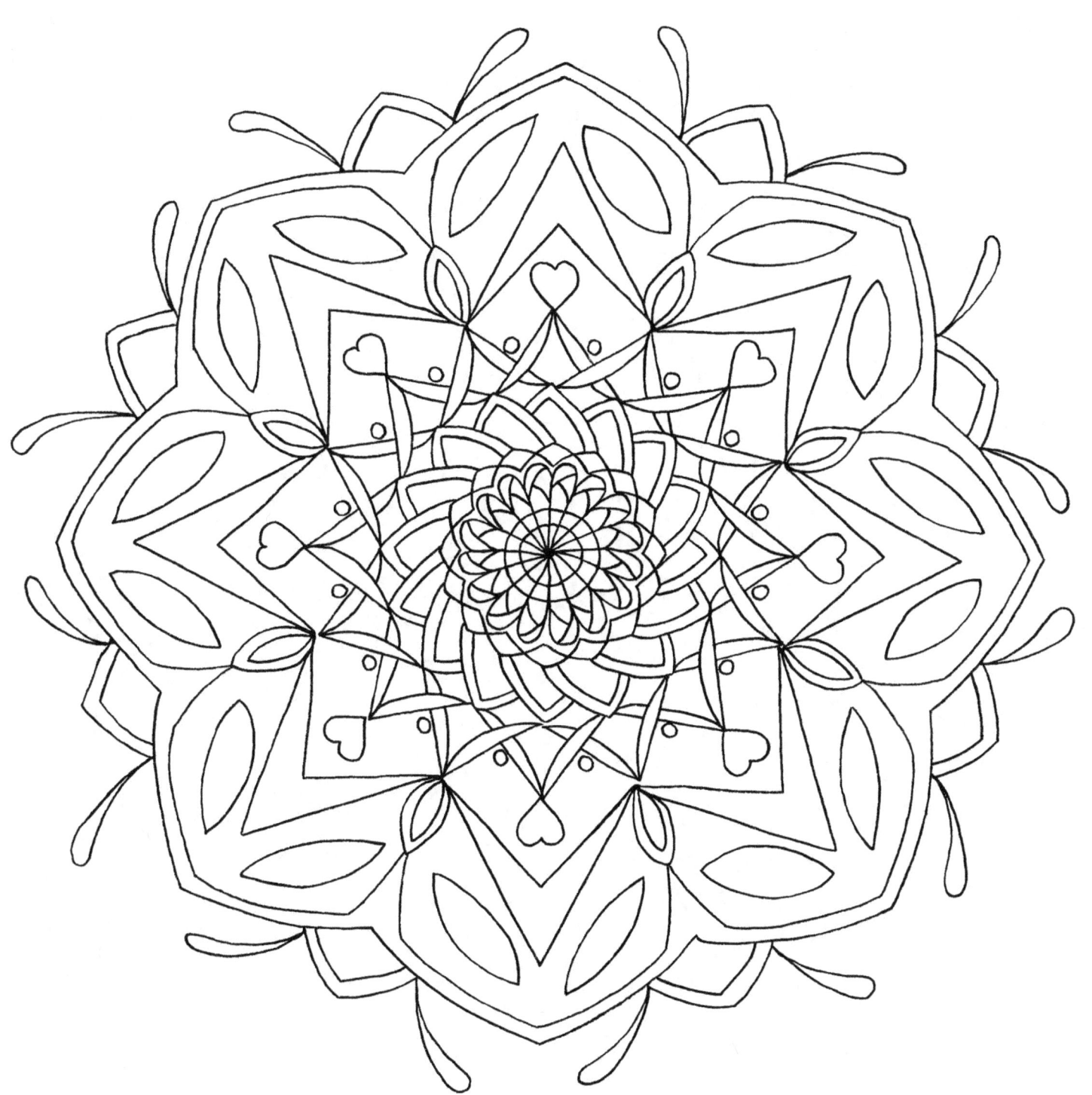

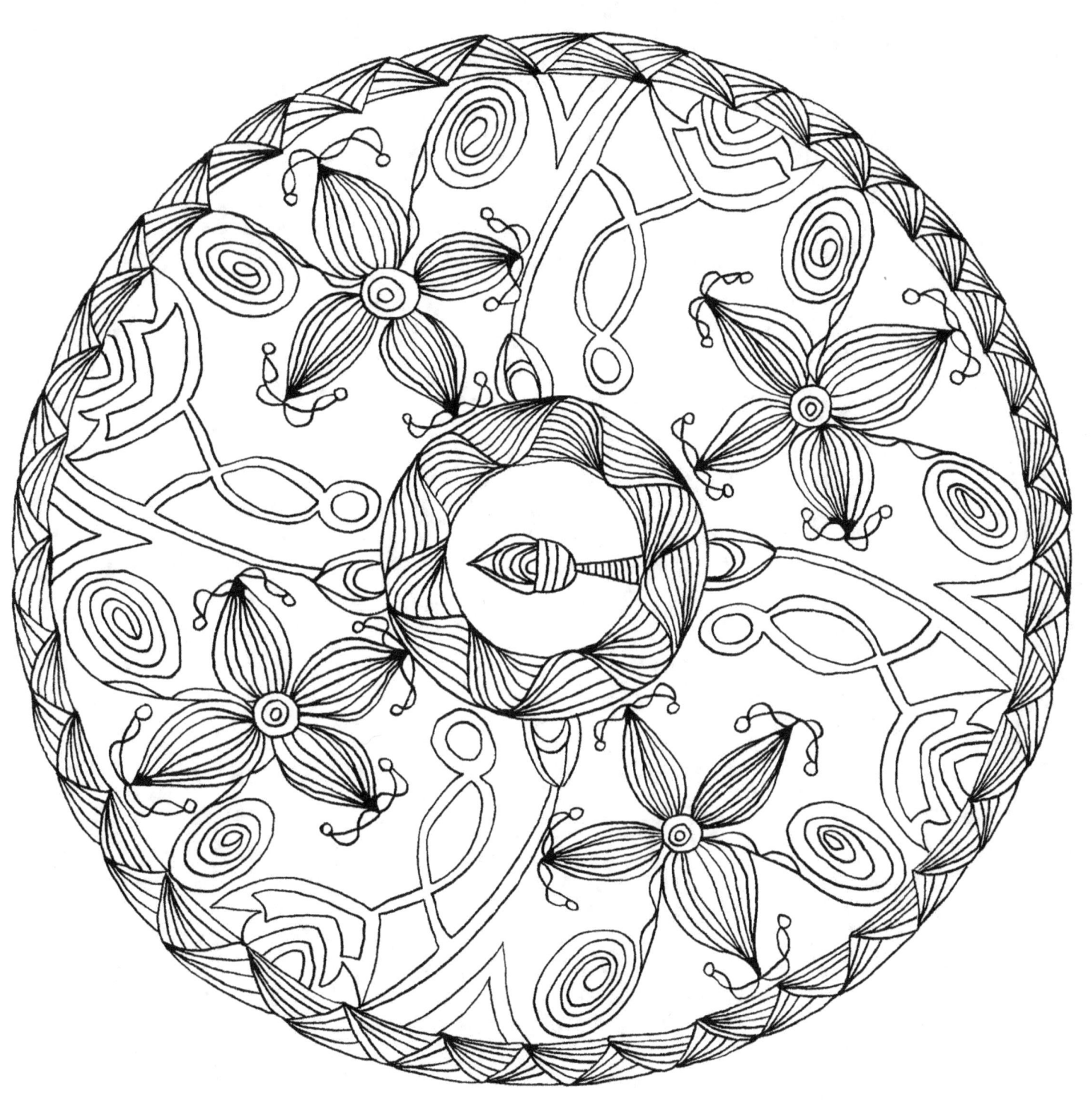

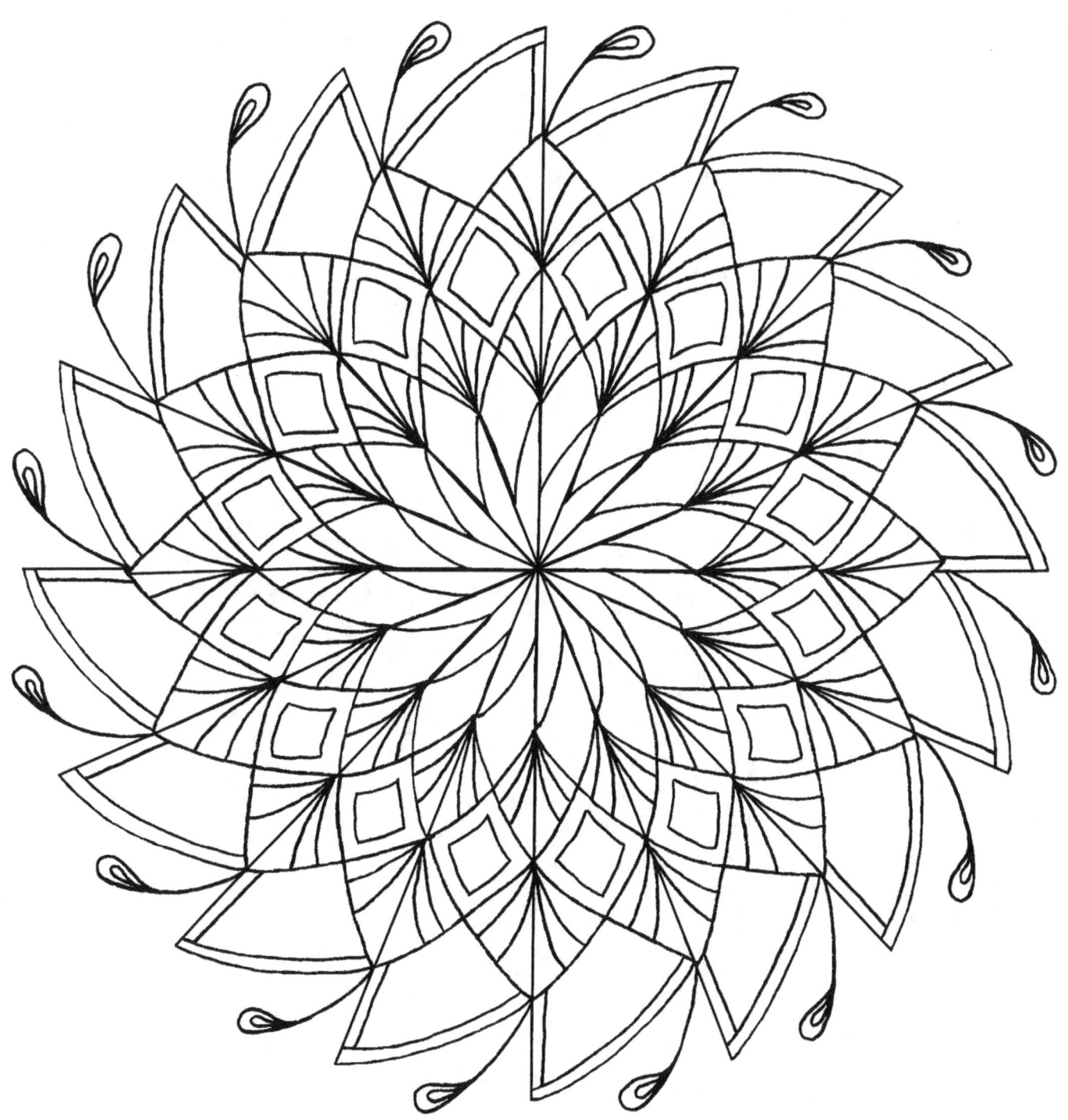

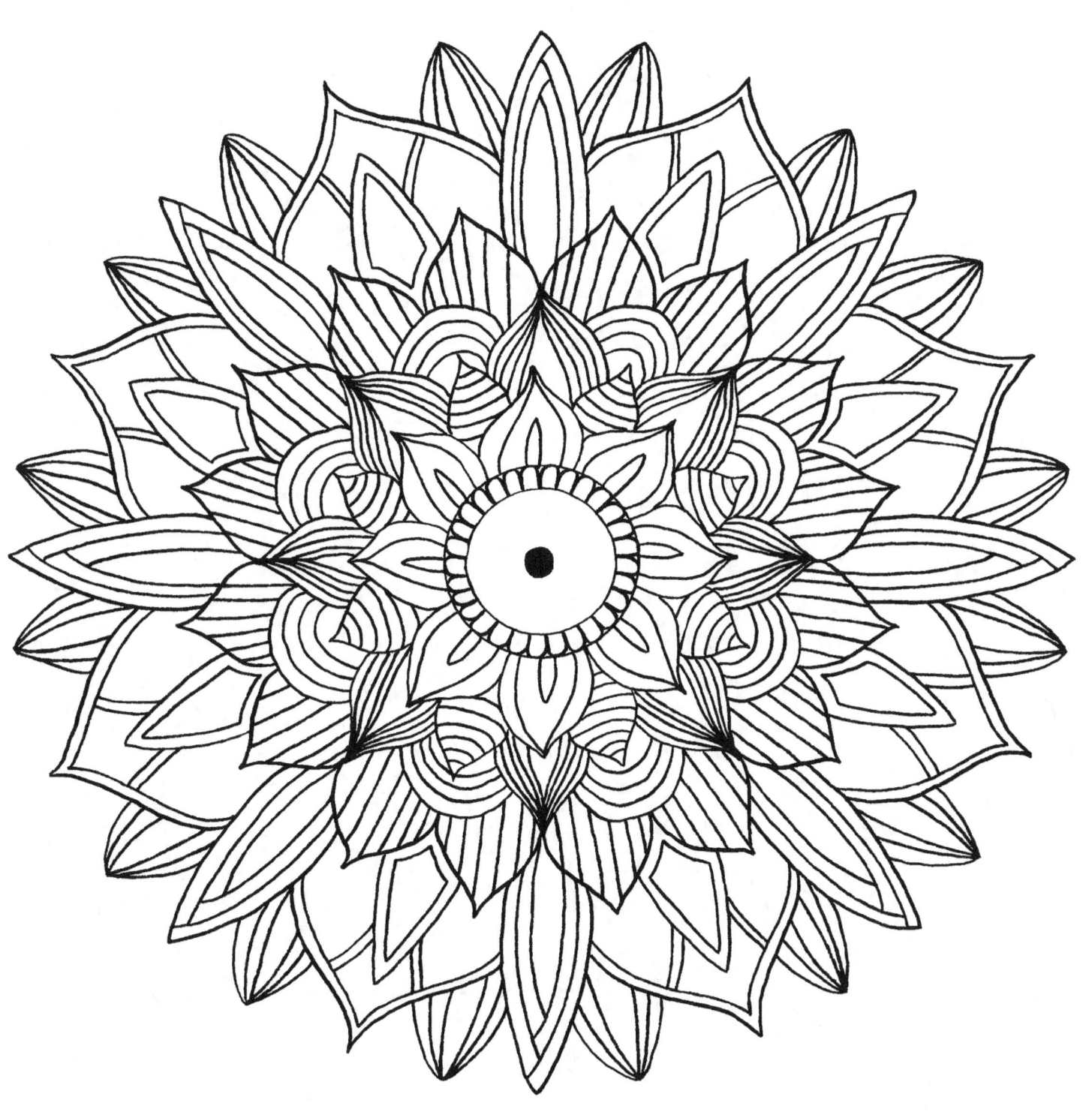

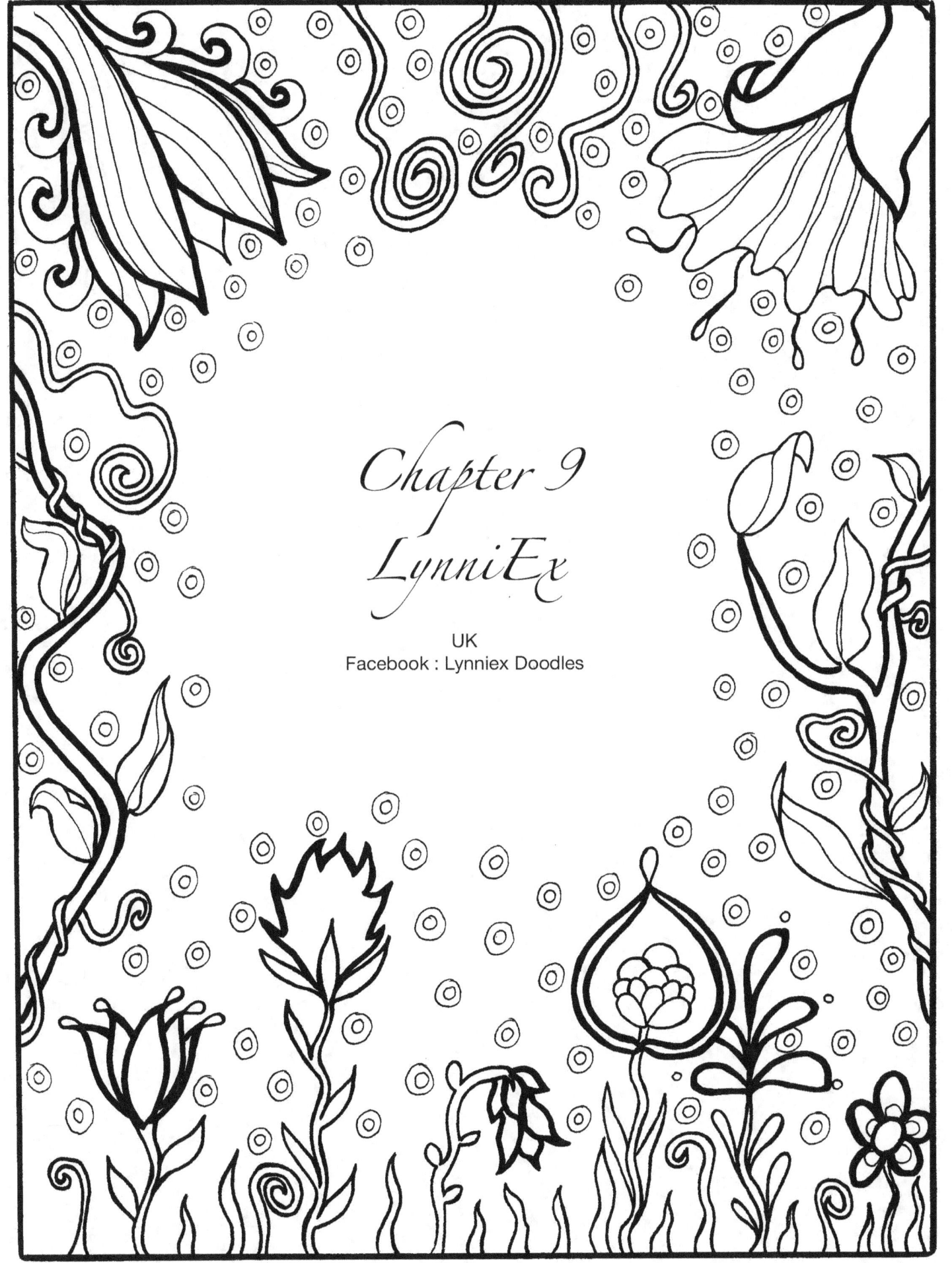

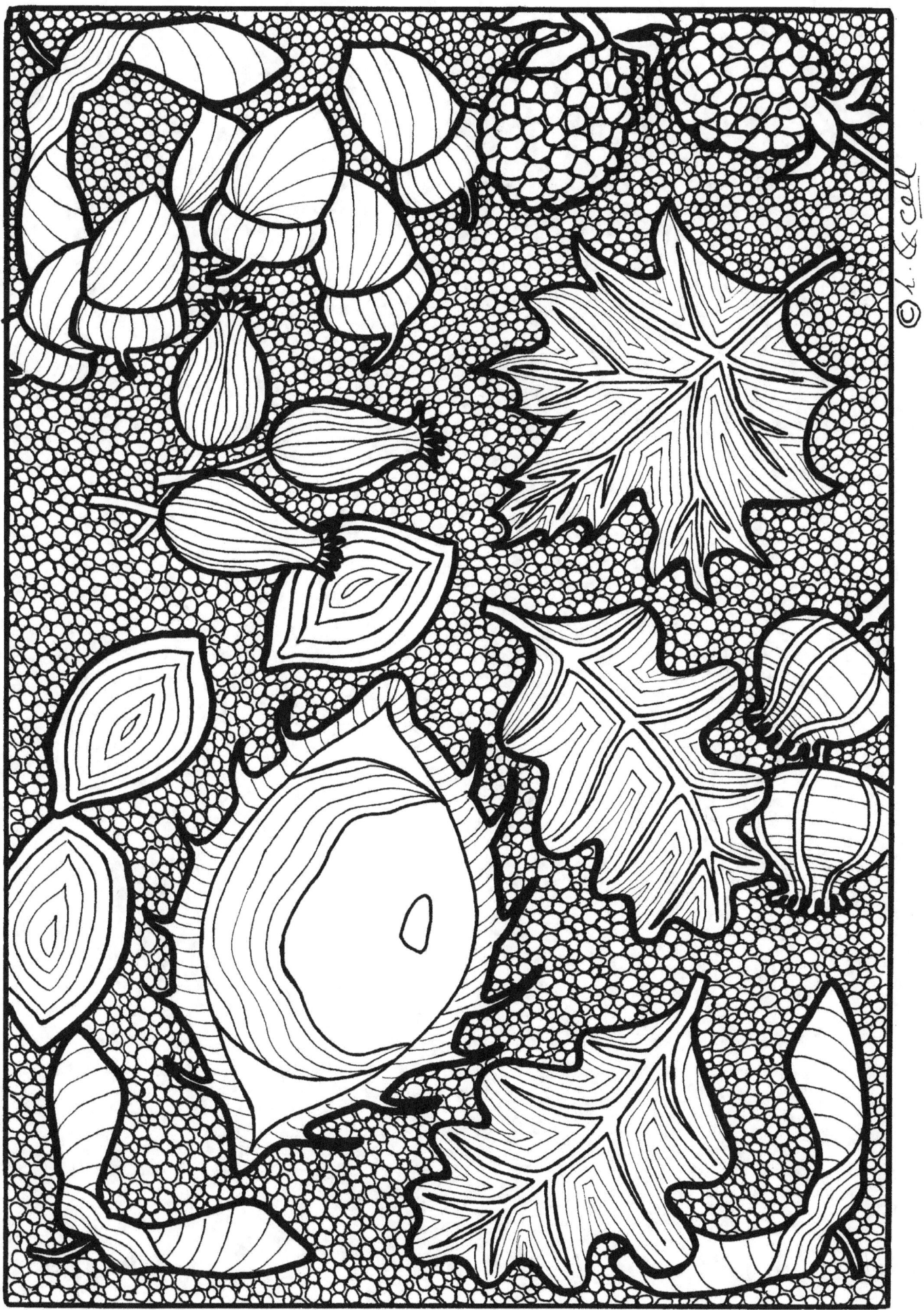

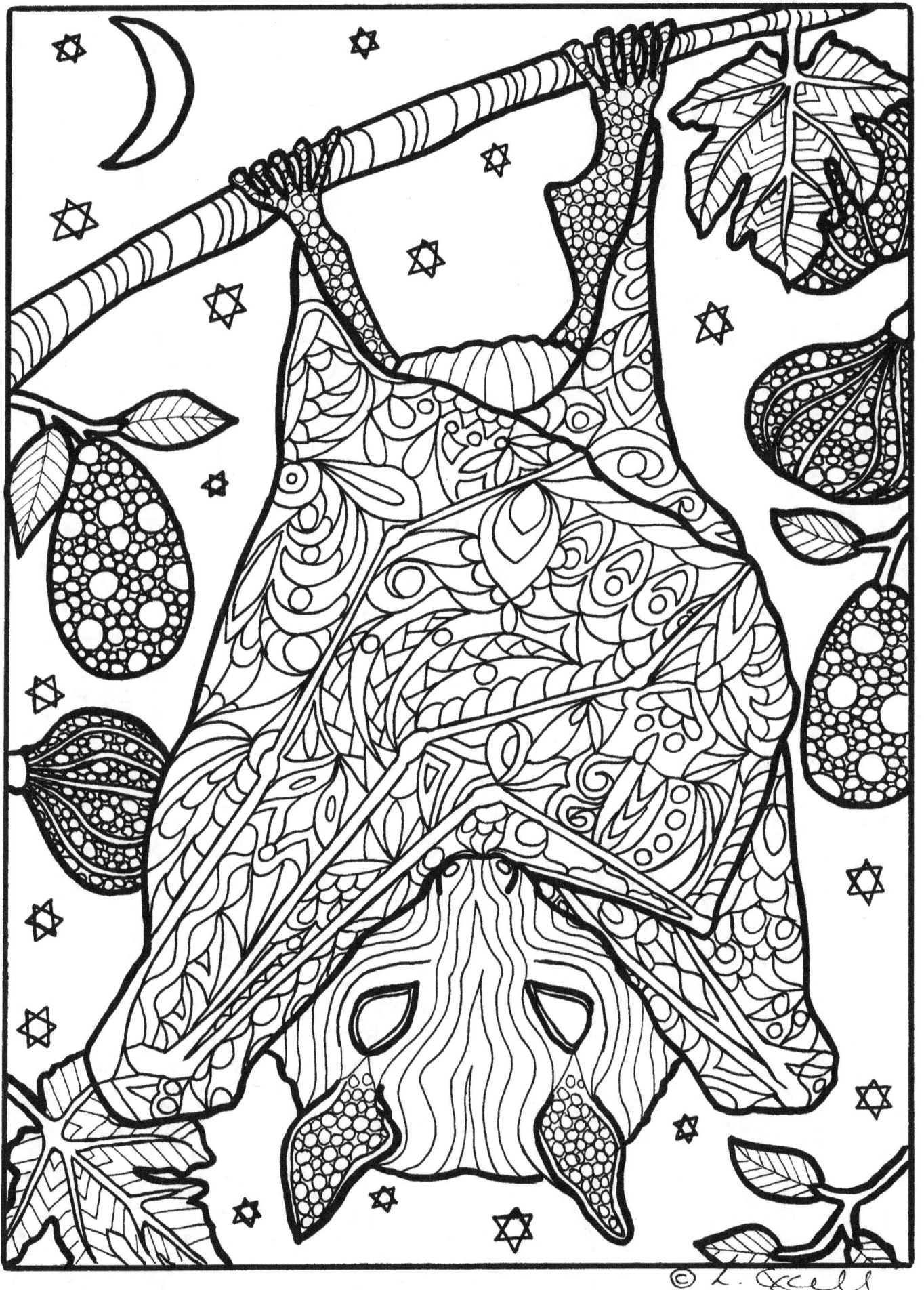

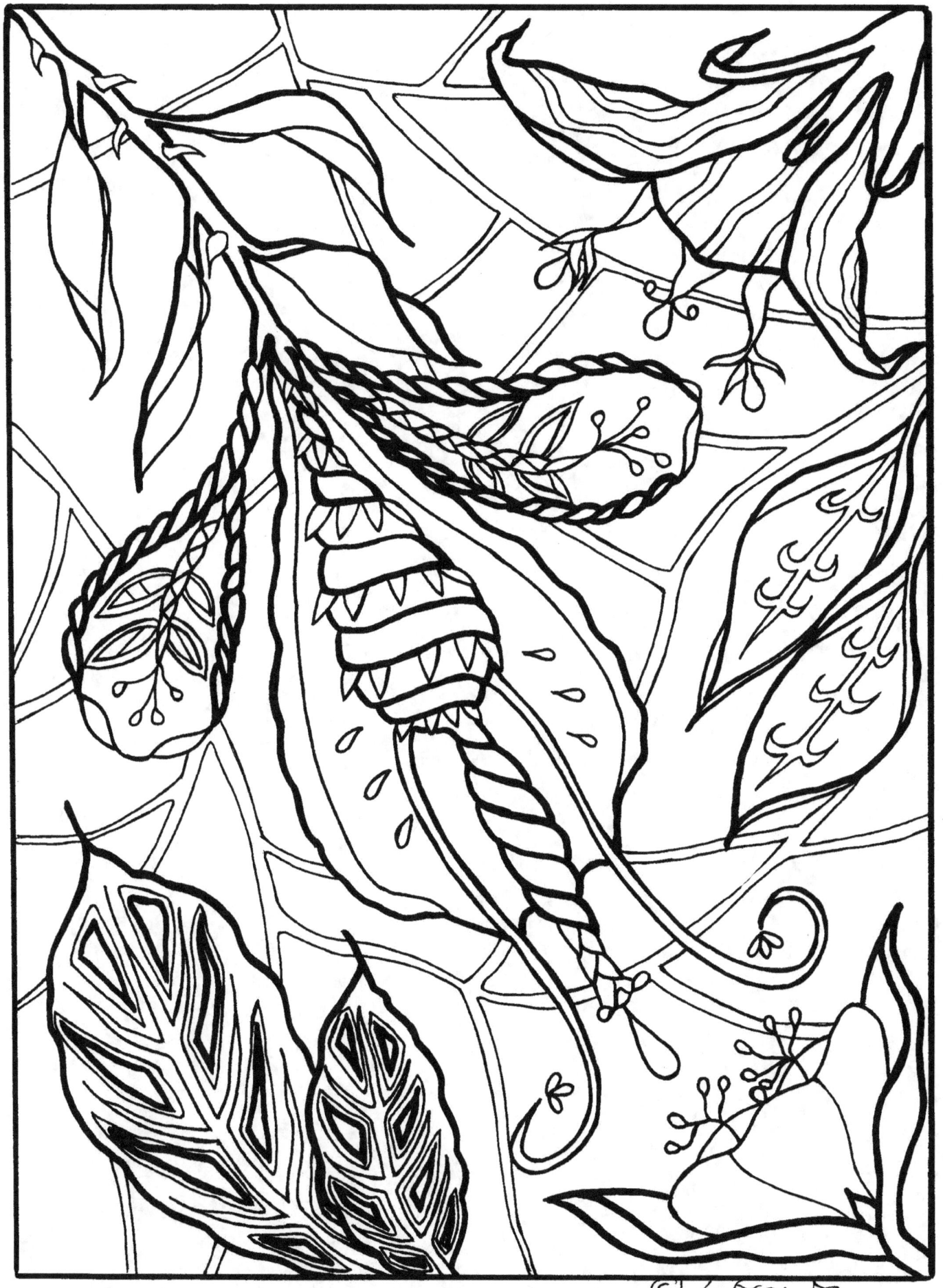

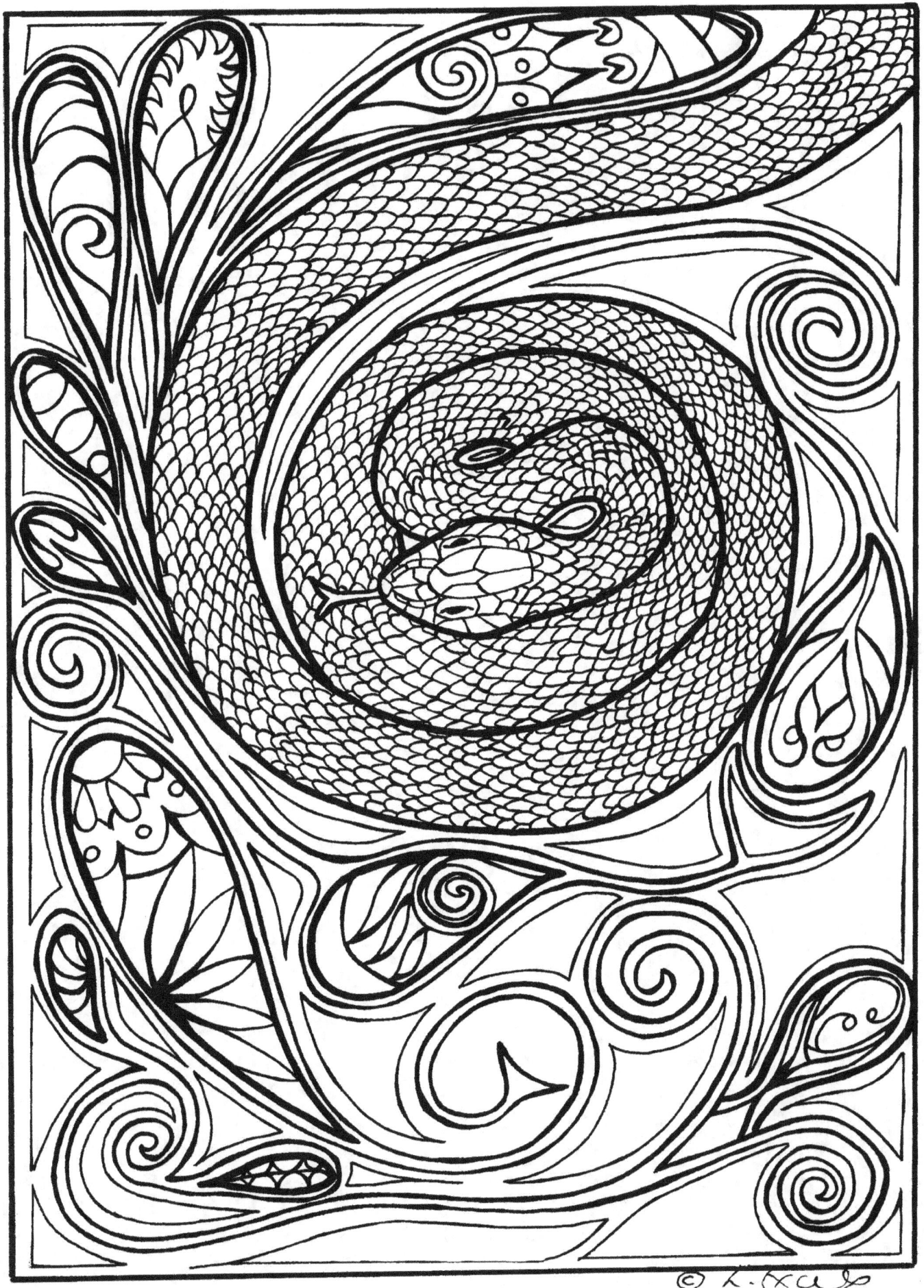

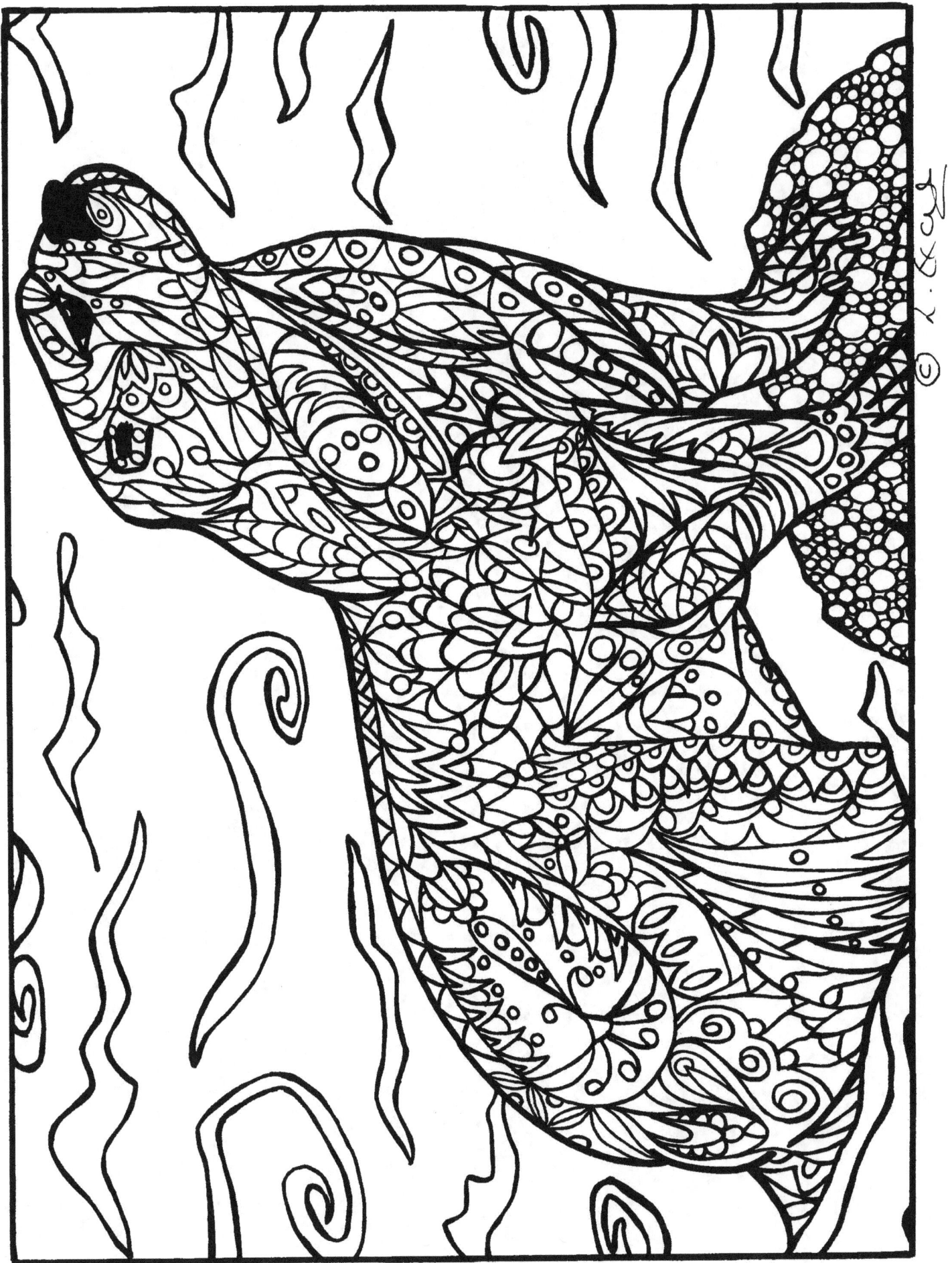

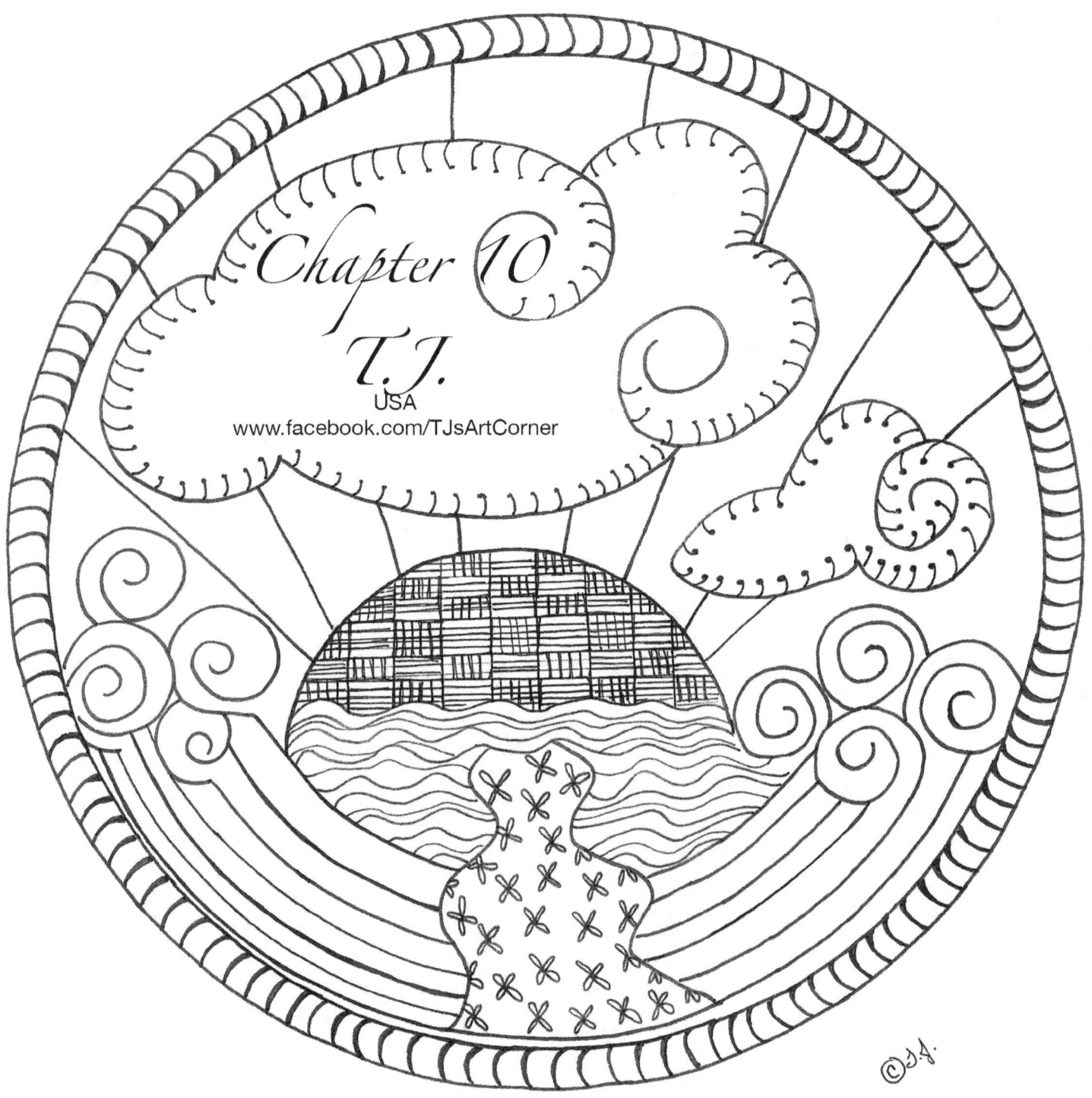

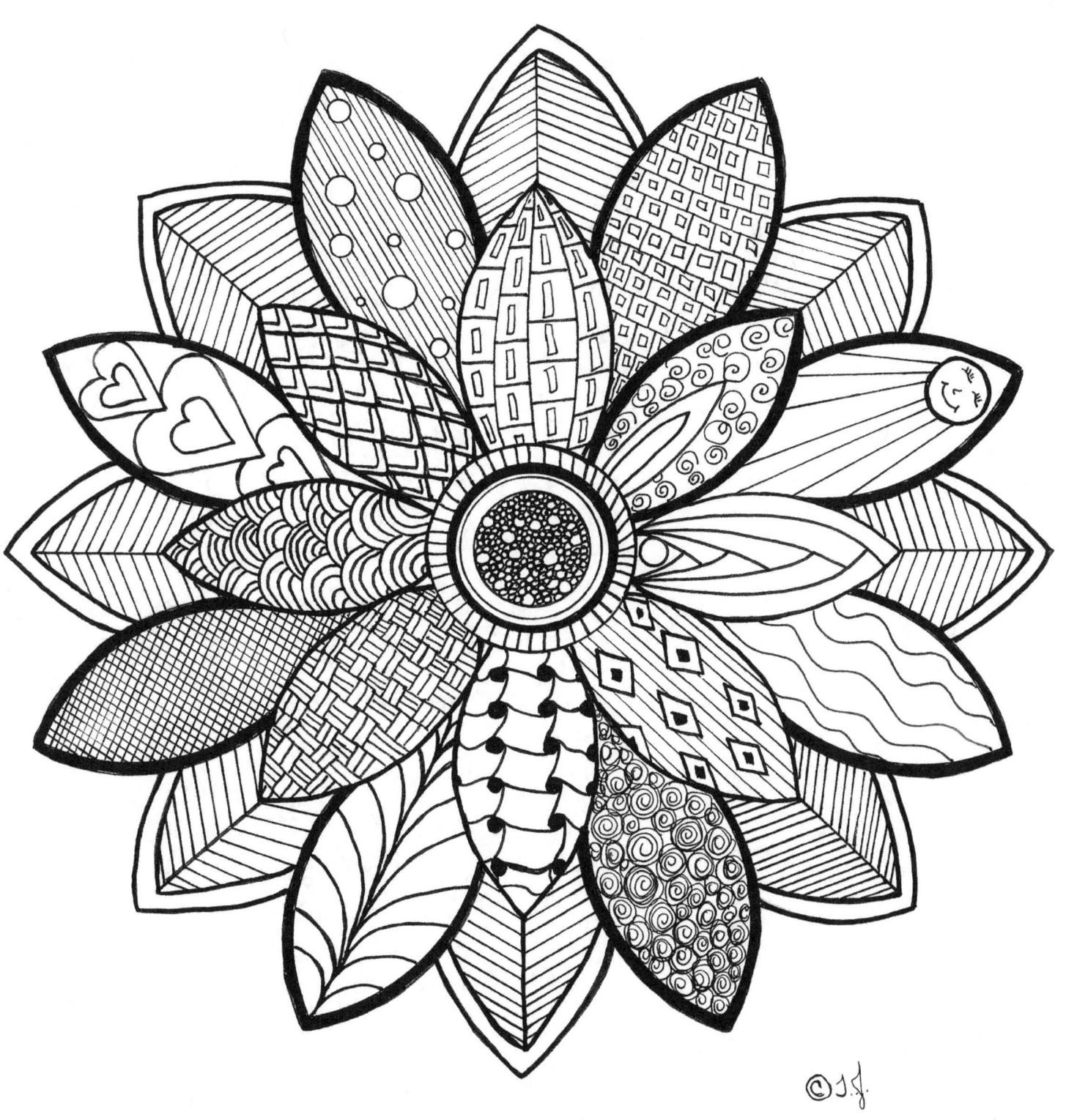

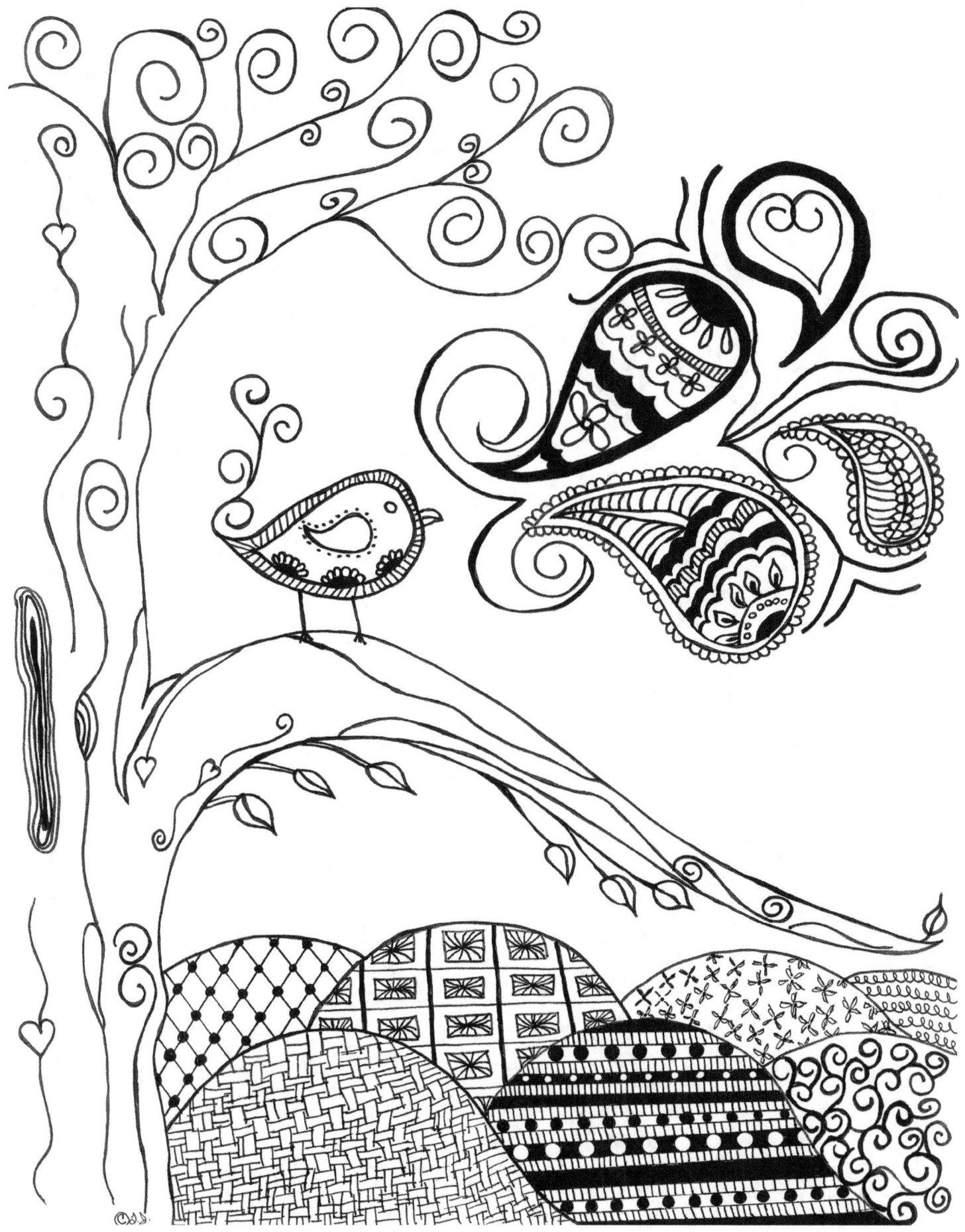

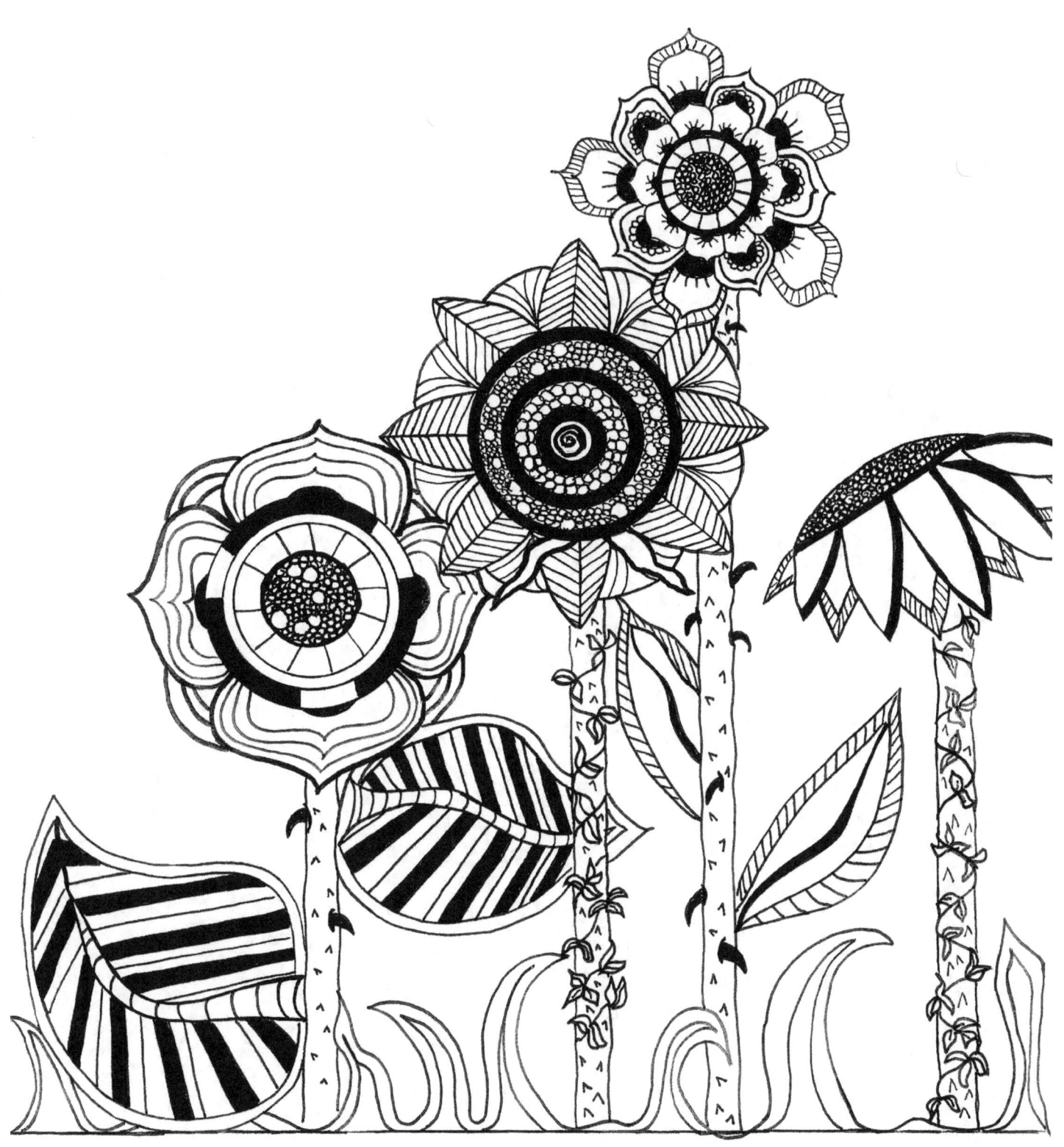

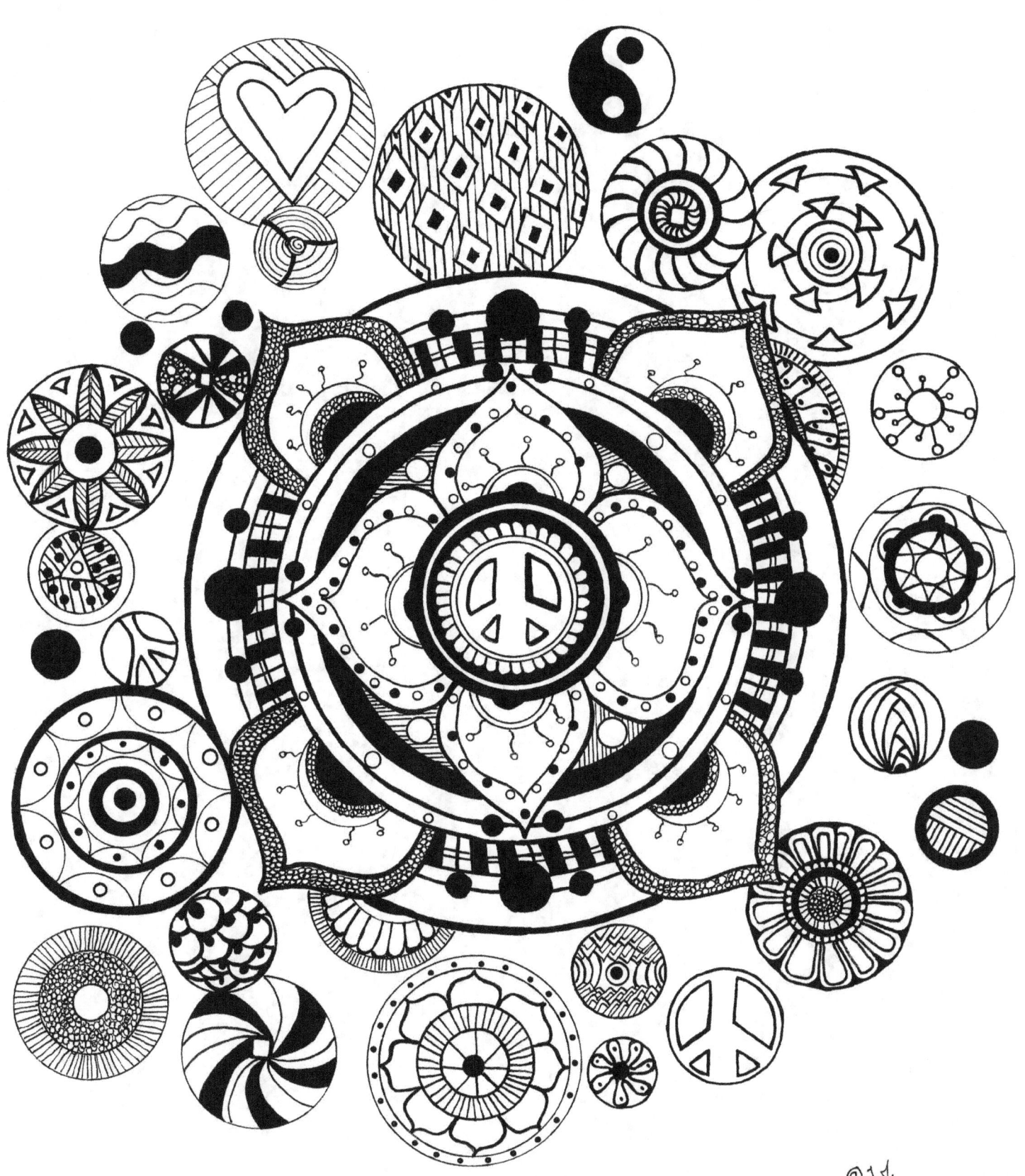

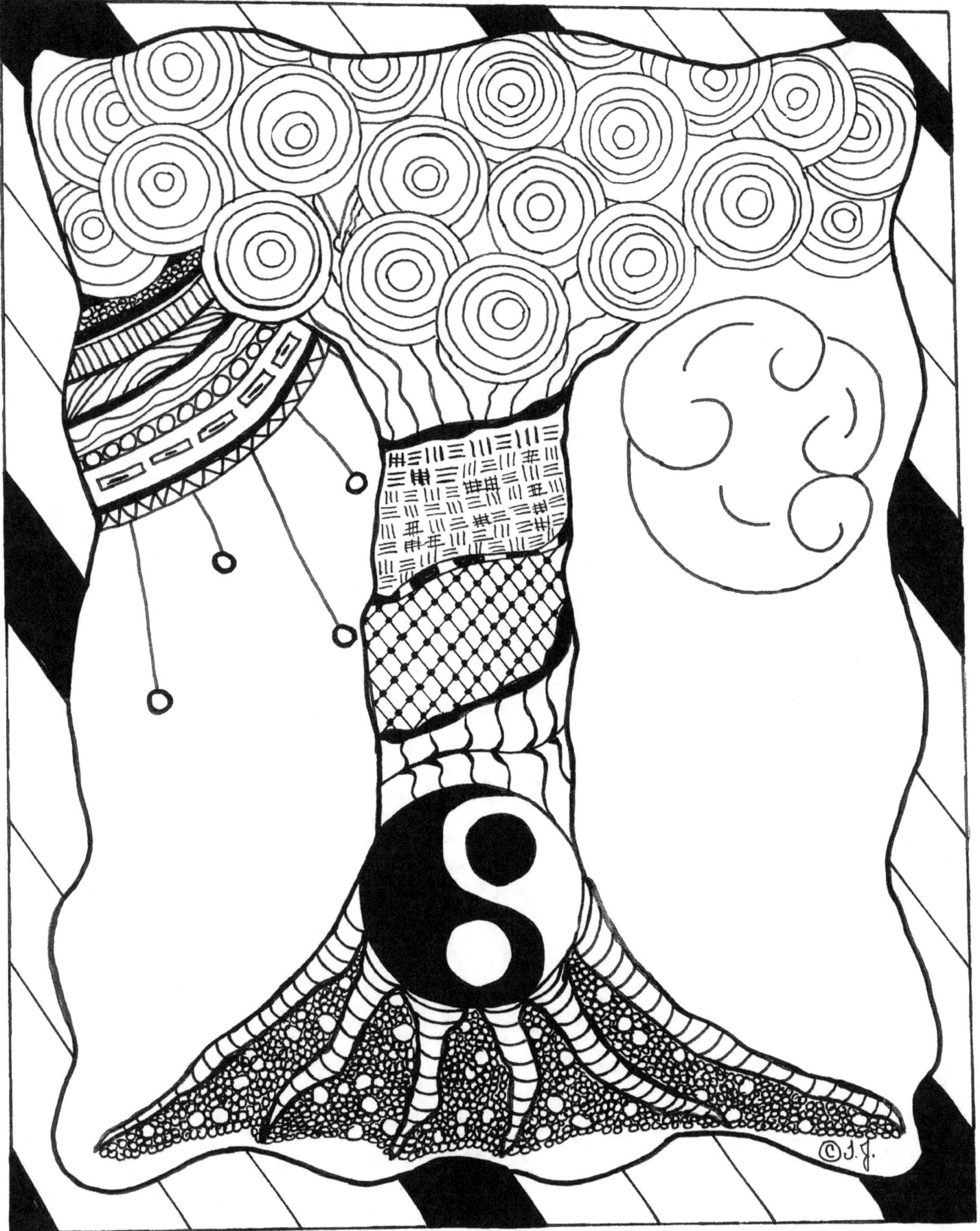

We from Global Doodle Gems, hope your journey through our book has been a pleasant one!

Please feel free to share your colored versions with us here:

https://www.facebook.com/groups/globaldoodlegems/

In our group you can meet the artists and enjoy exclusive freebies, video previews and participate in our community charity books "100 Doodles from 100 Doodlers" and so much more.... if you are wishing, that you could have the Chapter pages without the text, well then swing on by the group and get them for free in the freebie pdf for volume 5.....

Are you curious about Volume 6?....well, just take a look at the next 2 pages and you will know what to exspect in the next volume of "Global Doodle Gems!

"Global Doodle Gems" Volume 6
Preview

Joseph Shivery

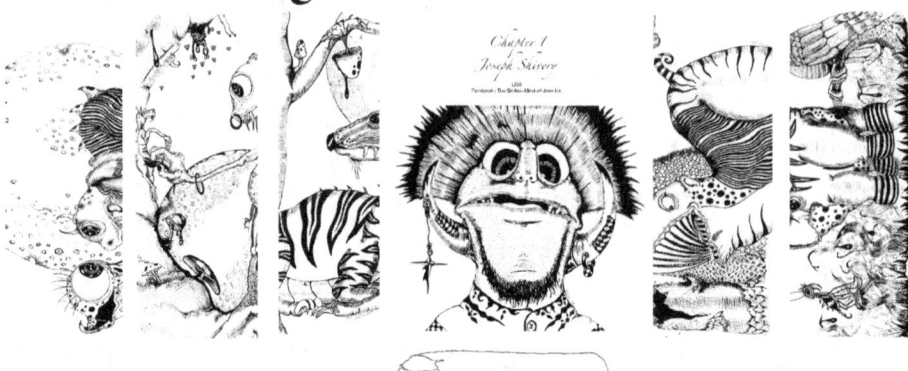

Nancy Sutton Lewin

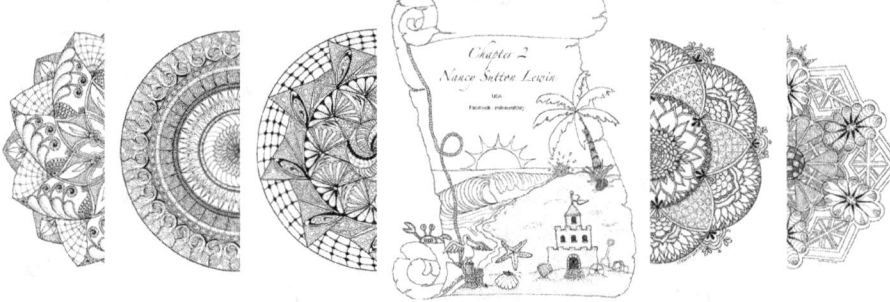

Mr End

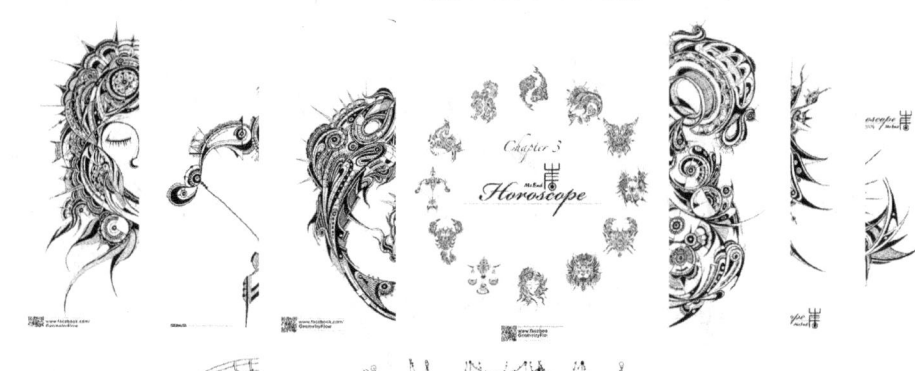

Diane Pick-Ross

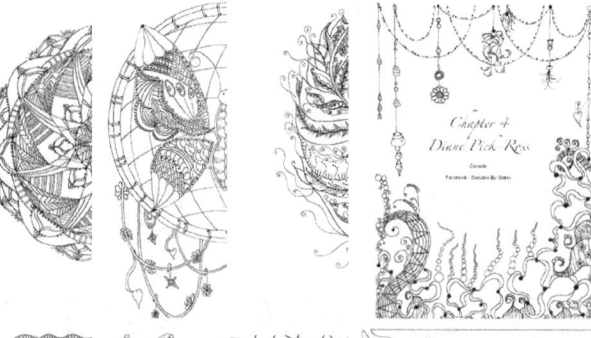

Judy West

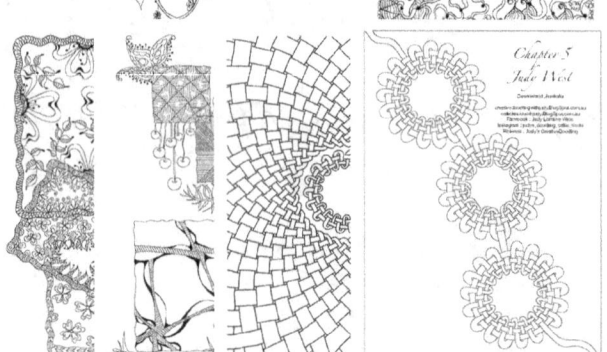

Arthur Santiago Quirat

Shelly Eartha Simpson

Dawn Miller

Alexandra Rodriguez

Laurie Beauchamp

Meet the artists feautured in "GDG" Volume 6

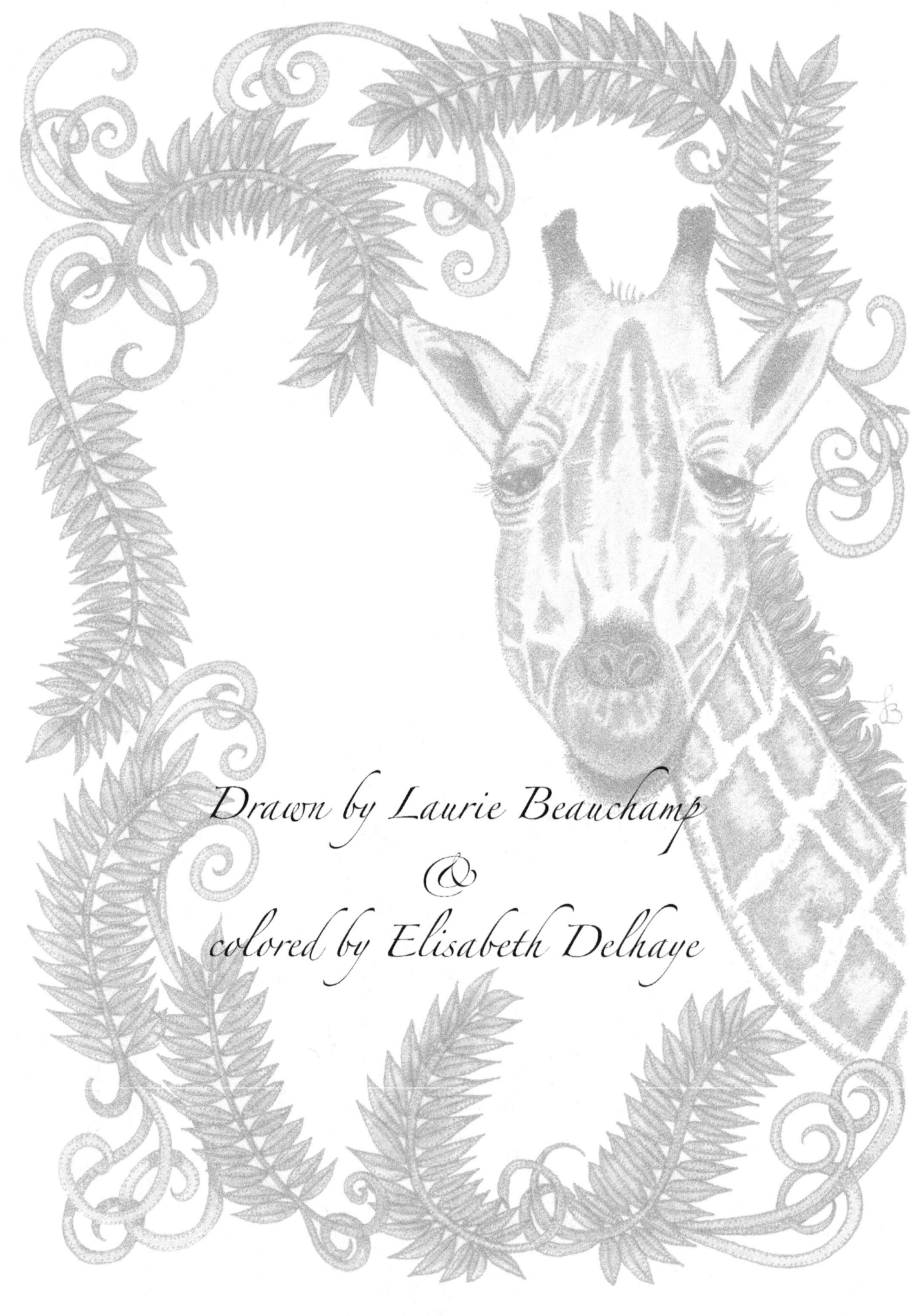

www.ingramcontent.com/pod-product-compliance
Lightning Source LLC
Chambersburg PA
CBHW082207220526
45470CB00010B/3076